PRENTICE HALL LITERATURE

PENGUIN EDITION

Teaching Resources

Unit 1
Origins and Traditions

World Masterpieces

Upper Saddle River, New Jersey
Boston, Massachusetts

ISBN 0-13-165186-2

1 2 3 4 5 6 7 8 9 10 09 08 07 06 05

Contents

UNIT 1

from the Bible: Book of Ruth
Psalms 8, 19, 23, and 137

from the Qur'an

from *The Thousand and One Nights:* "The Fisherman and the Jinnee"

from the *Rubáiyát* by Omar Khayyám

from the *Gulistan:* from "The Manners of Kings" by Sa'di

"Elephant in the Dark," "Two Kinds of Intelligence," "The Guest House," and "Which Is Worth More?" by Rumi

African Proverbs

from *Sundiata: An Epic of Old Mali*

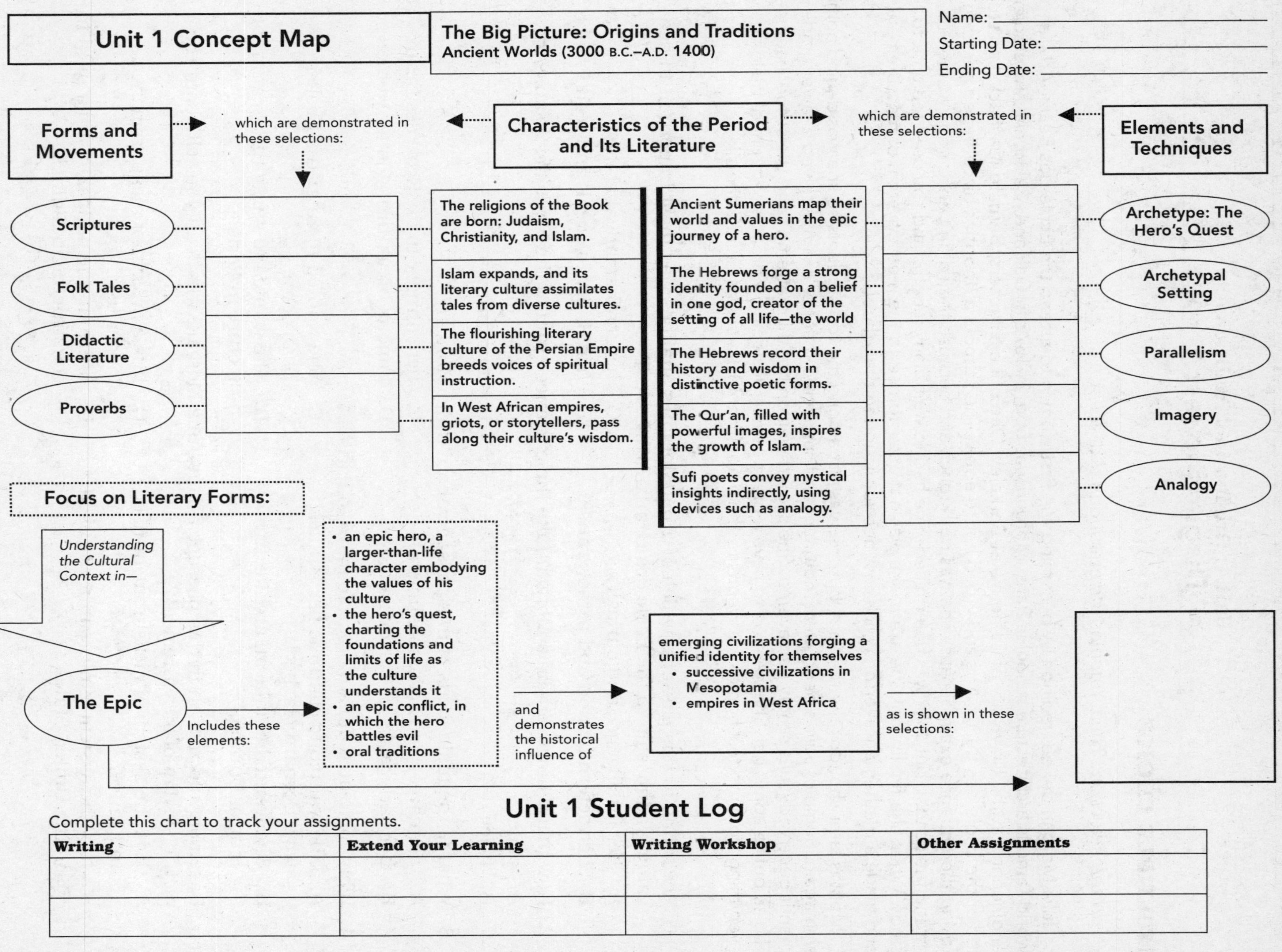
Unit 1 Concept Map
The Big Picture: Origins and Traditions
Ancient Worlds (3000 B.C.–A.D. 1400)
Name:
Starting Date:
Ending Date:
Forms and Movements
which are demonstrated in these selections:
Scriptures
Folk Tales
Didactic Literature
Proverbs
Characteristics of the Period and Its Literature
The religions of the Book are born: Judaism, Christianity, and Islam.
Islam expands, and its literary culture assimilates tales from diverse cultures.
The flourishing literary culture of the Persian Empire breeds voices of spiritual instruction.
In West African empires, griots, or storytellers, pass along their culture's wisdom.
Ancient Sumerians map their world and values in the epic journey of a hero.
The Hebrews forge a strong identity founded on a belief in one god, creator of the setting of all life—the world
The Hebrews record their history and wisdom in distinctive poetic forms.
The Qur'an, filled with powerful images, inspires the growth of Islam.
Sufi poets convey mystical insights indirectly, using devices such as analogy.
which are demonstrated in these selections:
Elements and Techniques
Archetype: The Hero's Quest
Archetypal Setting
Parallelism
Imagery
Analogy
Focus on Literary Forms:
Understanding the Cultural Context in—
The Epic
Includes these elements:
• an epic hero, a larger-than-life character embodying the values of his culture
• the hero's quest, charting the foundations and limits of life as the culture understands it
• an epic conflict, in which the hero battles evil
• oral traditions
and demonstrates the historical influence of
emerging civilizations forging a unified identity for themselves
• successive civilizations in Mesopotamia
• empires in West Africa
as is shown in these selections:

Unit 1 Student Log

Complete this chart to track your assignments.

Writing	Extend Your Learning	Writing Workshop	Other Assignments

Name ______________________ Date ______________

Unit 1: Origins and Traditions
Diagnostic Test 1

MULTIPLE CHOICE

Read the selection. Then, answer the questions that follow.

Julia Morgan defied tradition by becoming the first woman to attend the Ecole des Beaux-Arts, a world-famous architecture school in Paris. Morgan was born in 1872 in Oakland, California, and studied engineering at the University of California at Berkeley. One of her teachers, Bernard Maybeck, had studied at the Ecole des Beaux-Arts and urged her to apply. The school's authorities discouraged her from taking the entrance exam because she was not French and because they didn't encourage women to attend the school, but Julia was determined. She had to wait many months and she used the time to study. When she finally took the exam, she was not accustomed to the metric system of measurements and made a mathematical error, which cost her admission to the school.

Months later she took the re-exam, but she was not among the top students so she was denied admission again. Some of Julia's peers were indignant and suspected that her exam received a lower grade than it deserved. Julia simply persevered. She scored well on her third attempt and the school had no choice but to admit her. She went on to have a great career, designing a broad spectrum of buildings, everything from modest homes for friends to the magnificent Hearst Castle in California.

1. According to this passage, which of Julia Morgan's qualities was most important in her gaining admission to the Ecole des Beaux-Arts?

A. her intelligence and curiosity
B. her determination and perseverance
C. her mathematical ability
D. her ability to speak and read French

2. How many times did Julia Morgan take the entrance exam to the Ecole des Beaux-Arts?

A. once
B. twice
C. three times
D. four times

3. What is the main focus of this passage about Julia Morgan?

A. her career and accomplishments
B. her early years in California
C. her entrance to the Ecole des Beaux-Arts
D. famous breakthroughs for women

4. What motivated Julia Morgan to move to Paris?

A. She wanted to continue her studies with Bernard Maybeck.
B. She wanted to take an architectural tour of Europe.
C. She wanted to enter the Ecole des Beaux-Arts.
D. She wanted to study the great architecture in Paris.

5. Based on information in this passage about Julia Morgan, what can you tell about the metric system of measurement?

A. It is the system of measurement used in France.
B. It is the system of measurement used in the United States.
C. It is a system of measurement no longer used today.
D. It is a mathematical formula used in constructing buildings.

Name ______________________________ Date ______________

6. What is the organizational pattern of the passage about Julia Morgan?
   - A. spatial order
   - B. order of importance
   - C. chronological order
   - D. cause-effect order

7. Based on information in this passage about Julia Morgan, which of the following statements about the position of women in the late nineteenth century is true?
   - A. Women were treated as equal to men and were free to pursue any career.
   - B. Not all careers were open to women.
   - C. There were just as many women working as architects as men.
   - D. Women were legally prohibited from entering certain careers.

Read the selection. Then, answer the questions that follow.

Gumption and determination are words often used to describe Thurgood Marshall, who was the first African American Supreme Court Justice (1967–1991). Marshall was born in Baltimore, Maryland, in 1908, a time when African Americans were kept separate from whites in much of American society and were often treated with contempt. For his undergraduate work, Marshall enrolled at Lincoln University, a black college. When he applied to the nearby University of Maryland's law school in 1930, he was rejected because he was an African American. Not to be deterred, Marshall resumed his efforts to enter law school and was admitted to Howard University, in Washington, D.C., that same year.

In his first major court case, Marshall sued the University of Maryland for failing to admit Donald Gaines Murray, an African American applicant with an excellent academic record. Marshall was able to prove that the school rejected Murray because of his race. When the court found in Murray's favor, the university was forced to end its restrictive admissions policy and to accept qualified African American candidates.

There were many such victories ahead for Thurgood Marshall. In his most famous case, *Brown* v. *the Board of Education of Topeka, Kansas* (1954), he energetically led the fight against segregation. The Supreme Court's decision in that case ended the legal basis for separating students by race in public schools throughout the country.

8. This passage focuses mainly on which of the following aspects of Thurgood Marshall's life?
   - A. his childhood
   - B. his philosophical beliefs
   - C. his career as a lawyer
   - D. his Supreme Court career

9. In his career as a lawyer, Thurgood Marshall fought against
   - A. ignorance
   - B. greed
   - C. injustice
   - D. determination

10. Why was the case of *Murray* v. *the University of Maryland Law School* a "sweet victory" for Marshall?
   - A. Donald Gaines Murray was a personal friend of Thurgood Marshall.
   - B. The University of Maryland had rejected Marshall because he was an African American.
   - C. It was the first case that Marshall had argued before the Supreme Court.
   - D. It was Marshall's first case as a Supreme Court Justice.

Name ______________________ Date ______________

11. Why did Thurgood Marshall sue the University of Maryland's law school?
    A. for rejecting him for a teaching position
    B. for ending its restrictive admission policy
    C. for not admitting him to law school
    D. for failing to admit Donald Murray

12. From context clues in this passage about Marshall, you can tell that *gumption* means
    A. boldness and enterprise.
    B. kindness and caring.
    C. creativity and curiosity.
    D. strength and humor.

13. Why was *Brown* v. *the Board of Education of Topeka, Kansas,* such an important case?
    A. It was Marshall's first major court case.
    B. It was a landmark case, establishing the principle of "separate but equal."
    C. It was Marshall's first case as a Supreme Court Justice.
    D. It mandated the end of racial segregation in public schools.

14. At the time of the decision in *Brown* v. *Board of Education of Topeka, Kansas,* Marshall
    A. was a law school student.
    B. had just graduated from law school.
    C. had been practicing law for 20 years.
    D. was a Supreme Court Justice.

15. Which of the following is the best title for this passage about Thurgood Marshall?
    A. "Thurgood Marshall's Life Story"
    B. "Thurgood Marshall: Fighter for Justice"
    C. "History of Racial Segregation"
    D. "Supreme Court Justice Marshall"

Name ______________________________ Date ______________

Unit 1 Introduction

Names and Terms to Know

A. Directions: *Match each name or term on the left with its definition on the right. Write the letter of the definition on the line before the name or term it defines.*

Names and Terms

___ 1. Mesopotamia

___ 2. Sumerians

___ 3. Hammurabi

___ 4. Nile

___ 5. Pyramid

___ 6. Hebrews

___ 7. Islam

___ 8. griot

Definitions

A. early Middle Eastern people who believed in one God

B. the storyteller in traditional African societies

C. Babylonian king who developed major legal code

D. the residents of Mesopotamia who developed wheeled vehicles and the earliest city-states

E. the sacred structure that housed the remains of the Egyptian pharaoh

F. the region between the Tigris and Euphrates rivers that saw the growth of the first major ancient civilization

G. the river along which ancient Egyptian civilization developed

H. a religion based on the revelations of the Prophet Muhammad

B. Directions: *Write an additional fact about each of the following names and terms:*

1. Sumerians: ______________________________

____

2. pyramid : ______________________________

____

3. Hebrews: ______________________________

____

4. Islam: ______________________________

____

Name ______________________________ Date ______________

Unit 1 Introduction
Focus Questions

DIRECTIONS: *Use the following hints to help you answer the focus questions. You will find all of the information in the Unit Introduction in your textbook.*

1. Why do you think that the legal code of Hammurabi played such an important role in the development of civilization?

   Hint: How were commercial transactions governed before the advent of the code? ______

   Hint: How were crimes defined and judged before the advent of the code? ______

2. List two or more reasons for the importance of the Nile in the development of Egyptian civilization.

   Hint: What impact did the Nile have on agriculture? ______

   Hint: What role did the Nile play in transportation? ______

3. What was the role of the griot in the literature of Africa?

   Hint: How did the griot help support the stable social order that made literature possible?

   Hint: How did the griot help carry on the cultural traditions that underlay African literature? ______

from **The Epic of Gilgamesh**

Vocabulary Warm-up Word Lists

Study these words from the selection. Then, complete the activities.

Word List A

abundance [uh BUN duhns] *n.* plentiful amount
We found an abundance of flowers in our neighbor's garden.

contend [kuhn TEND] *v.* assert; argue
At the trial, the prisoner will contend that he is innocent.

endowed [en DOWD] *v.* gave as a gift; granted some special quality or ability
Her mother was a singer, and she endowed Jane with great musical ability.

extinguished [ik STING gwisht] *v.* put out; destroyed
The firemen extinguished the fire by spraying water on it.

fulfilled [ful FILD] *v.* satisfied; carried out
I have fulfilled the requirements that I need to graduate.

spawn [SPAWN] *v.* produce; give birth to
The heavy rainstorms may spawn a flood in the valley.

transformed [trans FAWMD] *v.* changed dramatically
The workers transformed the old barn into a new recreation center.

worldly [WERLD lee] *adj.* sophisticated
She is worldly because she knows a great deal about various cultures.

Word List B

amiss [uh MIS] *adv.* in a wrong way
Your vacation will not go amiss if you plan far enough ahead.

anointed [uh NOYNT id] *v.* applied liquid to, especially in a ritual
The nurse anointed the patient's wound with a medicinal oil.

bailiff [BAY lif] *n.* court officer who maintains order
The bailiff called the court to order.

ballast [BAL uhst] *n.* something heavy that helps balance or stabilize
The ship's ballast kept it from tipping in the storm's high winds.

libation [ly BAY shuhn] *n.* something to drink
The party's host poured a libation for his guest.

livid [LIV id] *adj.* enraged; pale or red
The team manager became livid when he heard the referee's decision.

scorching [SKAWRCH ing] *adj.* burning hot
He burned his feet walking on the scorching desert sand.

uproar [UP rawr] *n.* noisy confusion
The children's noisy games put the room in an uproar.

Name ______________________________ Date ______________

***from* The Epic of Gilgamesh**

Vocabulary Warm-up Exercises

Exercise A *Fill in each blank in the paragraph below, using each word from Word List A only once.*

The garden is now filled with an [1] ______________ of wildflowers—gorgeous red, blue, yellow, pink, and white blossoms. We didn't expect last year's plants to [2] ______________ so many new ones this year, but there do seem to be more blooms than before. These flowers have [3] ______________ last winter's bare yard into a beautiful summer retreat. Young children don't hesitate to come in and smell the wildflowers, and no adult is so [4] ______________ that he or she can resist the garden's appeal. Unfortunately, some people did [5] ______________ that the city council planned to destroy the garden in order to build an office building. However, it was a false rumor, and we quickly [6] ______________ it. So far, we have been [7] ______________ with good luck. The city council has [8] ______________ its promise to us to leave our garden alone.

Exercise B *Answer the questions with complete explanations.*

1. Name one type of <u>libation</u> that people serve at a children's birthday party.
   ____
2. Explain how you would react if you witnessed a large <u>uproar</u> downtown.
   ____
3. What news would make you <u>livid</u>?
   ____
4. What would you do if things went <u>amiss</u> in a friendship?
   ____
5. If an iron is <u>scorching</u>, is the iron too hot or not hot enough?
   ____
6. If you <u>anointed</u> yourself with an oily insect repellent, what result would you expect?
   ____
7. If you worked as a <u>bailiff</u>, who might your co-workers include?
   ____
8. Why is <u>ballast</u> especially helpful in a ship during a storm?
   ____

Name ______________________ Date ______________________

from The Epic of Gilgamesh

Reading Warm-up A

Read the following passage. Pay special attention to the underlined words. Then, read it again, and complete the activities. Use a separate sheet of paper for your written answers.

Sumerian civilization developed in a region that is now part of Iraq. Originally called Mesopotamia, or "the land between the rivers," the area was located between the Tigris and Euphrates rivers. These rivers endowed the land with soil that was good for farming; as a result, this part of the world became known as the Fertile Crescent. A dependable food supply helped give rise to one of the world's first civilizations.

At its height, Sumerian civilization was made up of about thirty city-states. These city-states were, for the most part, independent of one another. Each city-state had its own ruler. Each had its own temple as well. In fact, each city-state began as a place where the god's temple was built. The people of the city-state believed that they had a special god who fulfilled the responsibility of protecting the city-state.

Each city-state kept its independence by growing its own food and trading goods with other peoples. The soil, watered by the rivers, produced an abundance of crops, including plentiful wheat, dates, barley, and various vegetables. The Sumerians were also worldly people. They traded goods with other cultures located as far away as the Persian Gulf.

Unfortunately, it was inevitable that the competition for territory and dominance would spawn conflicts among the various city-states. By the fourth century B.C., the political nature of city-states was transformed. They were no longer independent. The ruler of the dominant city-state was considered the king of the entire region.

Eventually, the Sumerian city-states were conquered by the Babylonians. However, although the independence of the city-states was extinguished, the influence of Sumer was kept alive. Many scholars contend that the culture of the Sumerian city-states became an important part of Babylonian society.

1. Why would the rivers have endowed the land with advantages for farming? What might a person want to be *endowed* with?
2. Underline the words that tell what responsibility the god fulfilled. If a person *fulfilled* all of his or her responsibilities, how might the person feel?
3. Circle the word that is a clue to the meaning of abundance. Tell what *abundance* means.
4. Underline the phrase that describes a worldly activity of the Sumerians. Use *worldly* in a sentence.
5. Underline the words that tell what would inevitably spawn conflicts. Tell what *spawn* means.
6. Underline the phrase that tells the way in which the city-states were transformed. Use *transformed* in a sentence.
7. Underline the word that tells what was extinguished. List a word that is an antonym for *extinguished.*
8. Underline the phrase that tells what scholars contend about the influence of Sumerian culture on Babylonian society. Tell what *contend* means.

Name ______________________________ Date ______________

***from* The Epic of Gilgamesh**

Reading Warm-up B

Read the following passage. Pay special attention to the underlined words. Then, read it again, and complete the activities. Use a separate sheet of paper for your written answers.

Like a bailiff keeping order in a courtroom, Grandpop lined up the ingredients for his lasagna: cheese in its special bowl and the spices neatly arranged. After a libation of sparkling water, he started to prepare dinner, explaining as he went along.

"All right. First, cook your ground beef. Just get it a little brown—using a low flame, not a scorching one—and add the spices. Then, mix the beef into the sauce and cook some more. Then, cook the lasagna noodles."

We watched as Grandpop did all the things he described. The best part was the way he stirred the long, flat noodles in the boiling water. The noodles bobbed up and down, like ships without ballast, swirling around Grandpop's spoon.

"Now," said Grandpop, "time to put everything together." The kitchen erupted in a minor uproar as we kids cheered and ran for the bowls. Each of us was in charge of one of the cheeses. This time I got mozzarella, my favorite. Grandpop anointed the surface of the baking dish with oil and added spoonfuls of sauce. He laid down the first layer of noodles. He helped my cousin spread the soft ricotta cheese. I sprinkled the surface with mozzarella, and my sister topped it with parmesan cheese. Then we repeated the steps.

"Now," said Grandpop, "clear the way to the oven." We stood aside as he walked very carefully, carrying the heavy dish across the kitchen. He was a gentle man, but we knew that he would be livid with anger if anything happened to his lasagna. Fortunately, nothing went amiss, and the dish slid safely into the oven. As Grandpop closed the oven door, we all smiled and looked forward to smelling the baking lasagna—almost (but not quite) as wonderful as eating this special treat.

1. Underline the phrase that tells what one job of a bailiff is. Use *bailiff* in a sentence.
2. Underline the words that suggest what libation means. Name a popular *libation*.
3. Underline the words that help explain what scorching means. When might the weather be *scorching*?
4. Circle the word that tells what seemed like a ship without any ballast. Tell what *ballast* means.
5. Underline the phrases that describe the uproar. Describe someone or something that often causes an *uproar*.
6. Circle the words that hint at what anointed means. Use *anointed* in a sentence.
7. Underline the word that is a clue to the meaning of livid. Explain what someone who is *livid* looks like.
8. Suggest what could have gone amiss as Grandpop carried the lasagna to the oven. Tell what *amiss* means.

Name ______________________________ Date ______________

from **The Epic of Gilgamesh**

Literary Analysis: Archetype—The Hero's Quest

An **archetype** is a basic plot, character, symbol, or idea that recurs in the literature of many cultures. An example is **the hero's quest,** a plot in which an extraordinary person goes on a difficult journey to find or do something important. For example, in the ancient Greek epic the *Odyssey,* the hero is on a quest to find his way home after years of fighting the Trojan War. In Arthurian legends, King Arthur and the Knights of the Round Table go on a quest to find the Holy Grail.

DIRECTIONS: *Use this diagram to analyze the hero's quest described in "The Story of the Flood" in* The Epic of Gilgamesh.

Outcome:

____

____

____

____

Steps taken to reach goal:

____

____

____

____

____

Purpose to quest:

____

____

____

____

Hero:

____

Name ______________________ Date ______________

from **The Epic of Gilgamesh**

Reading Strategy: Understand Cultural Context

Cultural context refers to the activities, beliefs, and customs of the characters in a literary work produced by a particular civilization. The more you understand about a work's cultural context, the more you will understand and appreciate the work itself. For example, if you understand something about the Sumerians' belief in many gods and goddesses, you can better understand why Gilgamesh builds temples for Anu and Ishtar, why he calls on Shamash to help him fight Humbaba, and so on.

One way to learn about a work's cultural context is to read background materials provided in introductions, footnotes, and other informational features. Another way is to use details within the work itself to glean information about the characters' way of life. As you read *The Epic of Gilgamesh,* look for details about the cultural context in descriptions and in the characters' words and actions.

DIRECTIONS: *Use the following chart to record details about the cultural context of* The Epic of Gilgamesh. *Include information about the time and place of the epic as well as the activities, customs, and beliefs of the characters. The left-hand column begins with examples.*

Cultural Detail	What I Learned
1. Writing methods	
2. Construction of cities	
3. Agriculture	
4.	
5.	
6.	

Name ______________________________ Date ______________

from **The Epic of Gilgamesh**

Vocabulary Builder

Using the Latin Prefix *sub-*

The Latin prefix *sub-* means "under," "lower," or "down." It occurs in the word *subsided,* which means "sank to a lower level" or "died down."

A. DIRECTIONS: *In the following sentences, replace the phrase in parentheses with one of these words beginning with* sub-: submarine, subtract, subterranean, subtitles, submerge.

1. Ms. Pai taught her class how to add and (lower the amount)__________________.
2. The (ship capable of operating under water) __________________ was torpedoed.
3. The film's (translated dialogue printed under the picture) __________________ were hard to read.
4. I plan to explore (underground) __________________ caves in Spain next summer.
5. Can you (put under water) __________________ this camera without damaging it?

Using the Word List

immolation	somber	ominous	teemed	subsided
succor	incantation	ecstasy	babel	

B. DIRECTIONS: *Write the Word List word that best completes each sentence.*

1. My great-grandmother joyfully recalls the __________________ she felt on arriving in America.
2. She came on a crowded steamer that __________________ with immigrants.
3. People from many lands made the ship a __________________ of voices.
4. Some immigrants were brightly dressed; others wore __________________ colors.
5. Doctors and nurses offered __________________ to those who needed help.

C. DIRECTIONS: *Write the letter of the word that is closest in meaning to the Word List word.*

___ 1. immolation
A. offering B. crime C. digging D. freedom

___ 2. incantation
A. silence B. chanting C. burning D. contradiction

___ 3. subsided
A. guarded B. fought C. dwelled D. dwindled

___ 4. ominous
A. threatening B. optimistic C. pessimistic D. oppressive

Name ______________________________ Date ______________

from The Epic of Gilgamesh

Grammar and Style: Commonly Confused Words—*in* and *into*

Be careful that you do not confuse the prepositions *in* and *into. In* refers to place or position, whereas *into* suggests motion.

Gilgamesh lived *in* the city of Uruk.

Gilgamesh went *into* battle to help his city.

A. Practice: *Write the preposition—*in *or* into*—that best completes each sentence.*

1. Gilgamesh is a king who lives __________ ancient Sumer.
2. Gilgamesh and Enkidu go __________ the cedar forest.
3. After Enkidu dies, Gilgamesh travels __________ search of the secret of immortality.
4. Was it __________ the time of the flood that Utnapishtim learned the secret of immortality?
5. The god Ea went __________ Utnapishtim's dreams to warn him about the flood.
6. Utnapishtim built a boat divided __________ nine sections.
7. After the flood, Utnapishtim released a dove, a swallow, and a raven __________ the sky.

B. Writing Application: *Follow the directions for each item.*

1. Write a sentence about Gilgamesh that uses the preposition *in.*

   ____

2. Write a sentence about Gilgamesh that uses the preposition *into.*

   ____

3. Write a sentence about Uruk that uses the preposition *in.*

   ____

4. Write a sentence about Uruk that uses the preposition *into.*

   ____

5. Write a sentence about Humbaba that uses the preposition *in.*

   ____

6. Write a sentence about Humbaba that uses the preposition *into.*

   ____

Name ______________________________ Date ______________

from The Epic of Gilgamesh

Support for Writing

Gilgamesh's quest for immortality might remind you of a quest by one of your favorite heroes from modern-day books, movies, or TV. Use the following chart to help you write an essay comparing and contrasting the quest of Gilgamesh to that of a modern hero.

	Gilgamesh	**Modern-Day Hero**
Nature or goal of quest		
Similarities in quests		
Differences between quests		
Successes of hero		
Failures of hero		
Outcome of quest		
Lesson to be learned from quest (if any)		

Now, use your notes to write an essay comparing and contrasting the quests of Gilgamesh and of the hero you have chosen.

Name ______________________________ Date ______________

from **The Epic of Gilgamesh**

Support for Extend Your Learning

Research and Technology

Use the following chart as an aid in organizing your **research report** about the rediscovery of *Gilgamesh* in the nineteenth century. Jot down answers to the key questions on the basis of your initial research. Use these preliminary notes as a guide to raising further relevant questions and pursuing any additional needed research. Then, organize your notes into a thorough, informative report that you can present to the class.

Key Questions to Guide Research
Where and when was the rediscovery made?
In what form was *Gilgamesh* preserved?
What other poems or stories about Gilgamesh have survived?

Listening and Speaking

Use the lines below to jot down ideas for the questions reporters might ask Gilgamesh in a **press conference.** Then, write the answers to those questions that might be given by Gilgamesh or his advisers.

Possible questions to ask Gilgamesh:

1. ______________________________
2. ______________________________
3. ______________________________
4. ______________________________
5. ______________________________

Possible answers to questions:

1. ______________________________
2. ______________________________
3. ______________________________
4. ______________________________
5. ______________________________

Name ______________________________ Date ______________

from The Epic of Gilgamesh

Enrichment: Epics and Epic Heroes

An **epic** is a long narrative or narrative poem that focuses on the deeds of heroes. Early epics are sometimes called national epics because they are very significant to the nation or culture that produced them. They usually attempt to record historical events considered important by that nation or culture, even though fantastic or supernatural elements are often introduced. The epic hero is a cultural icon, or celebrated cultural figure, who usually enjoys an influential position in society and whose deeds often help to advance or preserve that society in some way. The qualities and talents that the epic hero displays reflect the values and beliefs of the culture that produced the hero, and the hero's flaws or limitations can also help reveal cultural attitudes.

Directions: *Answer the questions on the lines provided.*

1. What historical events does the selection from *Gilgamesh* apparently help record?

____

2. What is Gilgamesh's position in his society?

____

3. In what ways do Gilgamesh's deeds help advance or preserve that society?

____

____

____

____

4. What do Gilgamesh's qualities and talents suggest were important values in the ancient Sumerian and Babylonian cultures? What do his flaws or limitations show about ancient Sumerian or Babylonian cultural attitudes?

____

____

____

____

5. What positive qualities or talents do you think would be displayed by the hero of an epic produced in America today? What flaws might such a hero display?

Positive Qualities/Talents: ______________________________

____

Flaws: ______________________________

Name ______________________________ Date ______________

from The Epic of Gilgamesh
Selection Test A

Critical Reading *Identify the letter of the choice that best answers the question.*

____ **1.** What is the main purpose of the Prologue to *The Epic of Gilgamesh*?
A. to give a history of Gilgamesh's family
B. to tell about some of Gilgamesh's deeds
C. to tell the reader about the epic's author
D. to describe the ancient kingdom of Sumer

____ **2.** Which characteristic best explains Gilgamesh's feats of heroism in *The Epic of Gilgamesh*?
A. He knows Ishtar.
B. He is Enkidu's friend.
C. He has curiosity.
D. He is partly a god.

____ **3.** Which aspect of ancient Sumerian culture is evident in *The Epic of Gilgamesh*?
A. animal sacrifice
B. belief in one god
C. belief in many gods
D. faith in peace

____ **4.** Which statement from *The Epic of Gilgamesh* best describes the Sumerian view of war?
A. "He who leaves the fight unfinished is not at peace."
B. "O glorious Shamash, I have followed the road you commanded . . ."
C. "O Enkidu, should not the . . . captive man return to his mother's arms?"
D. "For myself I have gained nothing . . ."

____ **5.** Which statement is true of Enkidu in *The Epic of Gilgamesh*?
A. He has always been Gilgamesh's enemy.
B. He becomes Gilgamesh's friend.
C. He becomes Gilgamesh's enemy.
D. He is Gilgamesh's childhood friend.

Name ______________________ Date ______________

___ 6. After the defeat of Humbaba in *The Epic of Gilgamesh*, what quality of Gilgamesh's character is revealed when he asks, "O Enkidu, should not the snared [caught] bird return to its nest . . . ?"

A. cruelty
B. sense of humor
C. kindness
D. impatience

___ 7. Enkidu dies after telling Gilgamesh about his dream in *The Epic of Gilgamesh*. What does this event show about the Sumerian attitude toward dreams?

A. Dreamers have many wishes.
B. Dreamers travel to other worlds.
C. Dreams can predict the future.
D. Dreams reveal truths about families.

___ 8. What is the main goal of Gilgamesh's heroic quest in *The Epic of Gilgamesh*?

A. to defeat Humbaba
B. to build a boat to be saved from the flood
C. the search for the secret of immortality
D. to find a way to win the love of Ishtar

___ 9. In *The Epic of Gilgamesh*, which event causes Gilgamesh to set out on his quest?

A. the battle with Humbaba
B. the flood
C. Enkidu's dream
D. the death of Enkidu

___ 10. Which emotion best describes how Ishtar reacts to the flood's destruction in *The Epic of Gilgamesh*?

A. grief
B. joy
C. satisfaction
D. anger

___ 11. Gilgamesh says he has "gained nothing" at the end of the excerpt from *The Epic of Gilgamesh*. Why?

A. Power ruins all people.
B. Humans cannot fight death.
C. There is no place like home.
D. Great wealth can bring sadness.

Name ______________________________ Date ______________

Vocabulary and Grammar

____ 12. In which sentence is the word *succor* used **correctly**?

A. The rescuers provided *succor* to the flood victims.
B. The *succor* of the calculus exam frustrated Chan.
C. The players' families watched the *succor* match.
D. The soup's *succor* can be reduced by adding water.

____ 13. Which word best completes this sentence?

The tribal council began with a(n) _____ performed by the chief.

A. babel
B. immolation
C. incantation
D. succor

____ 14. Which sentence **correctly** uses the word *into*?

A. Humbaba lives *into* the forest.
B. Urshanabi schooled him *into* the secret of life.
C. Enkidu was afraid about to go *into* battle.
D. An epic is a story *into* which a hero has a quest.

____ 15. Which statement **correctly** states the rule for using the words *in* and *into*?

A. *Into* refers to position, but *in* suggests motion.
B. *In* refers to position, but *into* suggests motion.
C. *In* is a preposition, but *into* is a verb.
D. *Into* is a preposition, but *in* is a verb.

Essay

16. Write an essay discussing the strengths that make Gilgamesh a great hero in *The Epic of Gilgamesh.*

17. *The Epic of Gilgamesh* ends with Gilgamesh believing that he failed to achieve a major goal of his quest. In an essay, discuss the weaknesses in his character that might have contributed to this failure.

Name ______________________________ Date ______________

from **The Epic of Gilgamesh**

Selection Test B

Critical Reading *Identify the letter of the choice that best completes the statement or answers the question.*

____ 1. The main function of the Prologue to *The Epic of Gilgamesh* it to
A. tell about Gilgamesh's birth and family.
B. tell about Gilgamesh's background and feats, some of which the epic will later recount.
C. give the reader a better understanding of the poet-historian who composed the epic.
D. describe ancient Sumer, where the epic takes place.

____ 2. Which quality most clearly sets Gilgamesh apart from other Sumerians?
A. He is a faithful friend.
B. He shows compassion toward his enemies.
C. He knows how to prepare for a fierce battle.
D. He is part human and part god.

____ 3. Which cultural detail is most helpful in understanding Sumerian religious beliefs?
A. Enki was the god of wisdom.
B. Gilgamesh built a temple with brick.
C. Uruk was an important city.
D. The number seven was significant.

____ 4. Which statement best describes Enkidu?
A. He is a childhood friend of Gilgamesh's.
B. He starts out as Gilgamesh's enemy but winds up his friend.
C. He starts out as Gilgamesh's friend but winds up his enemy.
D. He is part man and part god.

____ 5. What is the main reason that Gilgamesh overcomes Humbaba in battle?
A. Enkidu coaches Gilgamesh's every move.
B. A scorching wind brings Humbaba to Gilgamesh.
C. The god Shamash uses his powers to help Gilgamesh.
D. Humbaba is a coward and runs from Gilgamesh.

____ 6. What important lesson does Gilgamesh learn after the battle with Humbaba?
A. A brave victory cannot ensure the pleasure of the gods.
B. Enkidu cannot be trusted as a friend.
C. Enkidu's advice should not be heeded.
D. The people of Uruk will never appreciate his achievements.

____ 7. Compared with Enkidu, which statement is true of Gilgamesh?
A. He seems more self-confident.
B. He seems humbler.
C. He seems more loyal.
D. He seems more thoughtful.

Name ______________________ Date ______________

____ 8. What is the hero's quest in *The Epic of Gilgamesh*?
A. Enkidu's confrontation with Humbaba
B. Utnapishtim's construction of a boat
C. Gilgamesh's search for the secret of immortality
D. Enlil's complaint of the din created by humankind

____ 9. What is the main event that prompts Gilgamesh's quest?
A. becoming king of Uruk
B. the death of Humbaba
C. the death of Enkidu
D. the flood

____ 10. How is Utnapishtim able to survive the flood?
A. The other gods prevent Enlil from hurting him.
B. Ea instructs him in a dream.
C. His immortality allows him to survive.
D. He begs Enlil to spare him.

____ 11. Why does Gilgamesh seek out Utnapishtim?
A. He knows Utnapishtim is the wisest man in the world.
B. He wants Utnapishtim to tell him how to become immortal.
C. He wants to learn how to survive a flood.
D. He wants to avenge the death of his friend Enkidu.

____ 12. Which character trait does Utnapishtim exhibit in the "The Story of the Flood"?
A. attention to detail
B. reliance on others
C. emotional reserve
D. extreme caution

____ 13. What does the archetypal nature of the hero's quest suggest?
A. It is a well-known plot too often repeated.
B. It somehow taps into widespread human desires.
C. Everyone familiar with quest stories will guess the outcome.
D. Quests are an important part of Sumerian religion.

____ 14. Which lesson do the quest and its outcome seem to impart?
A. Many a hero has followed a foolish quest.
B. Immortality, though rarely bestowed, is an important human goal.
C. Kings are nearly as powerful as the gods.
D. A human's desire for immortality cannot be realized.

____ 15. Which sentence from *The Epic of Gilgamesh* contains a detail most likely to help readers appreciate the cultural context of the work?
A. "I will tell the lady your mother all your glorious deeds."
B. "He slapped his thigh in scorn."
C. "'I made a sacrifice and poured out a libation on the mountain top.'"
D. "After twenty leagues they broke their fast."

Name ______________________________ Date ____________

Vocabulary and Grammar

____ 16. In which sentence is *teemed* used correctly?
A. After the bell rang, the hallway *teemed* with students.
B. The soccer *teemed* at the field at noon.
C. Is the main character brave, or is she *teemed?*
D. My baby sister cried constantly when she *teemed.*

____ 17. Which word below best completes this sentence?
The United Nations meeting was a(n) _____ of many languages.
A. babel
B. immolation
C. incantation
D. succor

____ 18. Which word contains a Latin prefix that means "under" or "down"?
A. incantation
B. ecstasy
C. immolation
D. subsided

____ 19. Which sentence does *not* use *in* or *into* correctly?
A. Humbaba lives *in* the forest.
B. Gilgamesh goes *in* the forest in search of Humbaba.
C. Utnapishtim leapt *into* the boat.
D. At the well, Gilgamesh goes *into* the cool water.

____ 20. Which statement correctly distinguishes between *in* and *into?*
A. *In* is a preposition; *into* is an adverb.
B. *Into* is an adverb; *in* is a preposition.
C. Unlike *in, into* is used to show motion.
D. Unlike *into, in* is used to show motion.

Essay

21. In a brief essay, analyze the heroic qualities that Gilgamesh possesses and those that he lacks. Cite examples from the epic to support your analysis.

22. In the story of a hero's quest, the goal must be an important objective, usually something that most people would like to possess. The quest then presents a series of hurdles or challenges that the hero must overcome to reach the goal. Sometimes the hero receives help from the outside; sometimes he or she does not. Write an essay in which you describe how *The Epic of Gilgamesh* fulfills or does not fulfill the conditions of a quest story.

23. What ideas and values were important to the ancient Sumerians? What did they expect of their rulers and heroes? How did they expect people to treat one another and conduct themselves in their daily lives? Answer these questions in an essay explaining what *The Epic of Gilgamesh* reveals about the values, morals, and standards of behavior of ancient Sumer.

Vocabulary Warm-up Word Lists

Study these words from the selections. Then, complete the activities.

Word List A

comprised [kuhm PRYZD] *v.* included; contained
That puzzle comprised five hundred pieces.

created [kree AYT id] *v.* made; produced; brought into being
The artist created a sculpture from scraps of metal.

devised [di VYZD] *v.* invented; arranged
Anne devised a plan to solve the problem.

expanse [ik SPANS] *n.* a wide open area
John could see the great expanse of forest from high atop the mountain.

fashioned [FASH uhnd] *v.* formed
We fashioned a bouquet from flowers that we picked in the garden.

midst [MIDST] *n.* in the middle position; center
I turned a corner and suddenly found myself in the midst of a street fair.

receded [ri SEED id] *v.* moved back; moved away from
The flood waters receded after the rain stopped.

terminate [TER muh nayt] *v.* bring to an end; conclude
The speaker will terminate his lecture promptly at five o'clock.

Word List B

abound [uh BOWND] *v.* to be plentiful
Come spring, tulips will abound in the area where we planted them.

array [uh RAY] *n.* an orderly arrangement
We chose our desserts from the array of treats that the waiter presented.

desirable [di ZYR uh buhl] *adj.* valuable; worth wanting
That painting is desirable because it is by a famous artist.

maintain [mayn TAYN] *v.* keep up; keep in a given condition
Susan had to maintain good grades in order to earn a scholarship.

renown [ri NOWN] *n.* fame; quality of being honored by many people
Thousands came to hear his speech because of his worldwide renown.

sprout [sprowt] *v.* grow or develop
The plants will not sprout unless you water the seeds.

vegetation [vej uh TAY shuhn] *n.* the plants of an area
John cleared much of the overgrown vegetation from his land.

vineyard [VIN yerd] *n.* a ground planted with grapevines
The vineyard contained several varieties of grapes.

Name ______________________ Date ______________

from the **Bible: "The Creation and the Fall"** and **"The Story of the Flood"**

Vocabulary Warm-up Exercises

Exercise A *Fill in each blank below with the appropriate word from Word List A.*

Looking at the great [1] ______________ of sky, we could see the storm coming toward us. Earlier, John had [2] ______________ an evacuation plan, and he based it on earlier plans that he had developed for similar situations. John knew that the evacuation plan that he [3] ______________ had to work. If it did not, many people would be caught in the [4] ______________ of the flooding that would result from the storm. The plan that John [5] ______________ was complicated. It was [6] ______________ of many parts. The plan included a requirement that all drivers immediately [7] ______________ their travel on the roads and seek shelter when the rain began to fall. When the floodwaters [8] ______________, John was both happy and relieved.

Exercise B *Answer the questions with complete explanations.*

1. What type of fruit is grown in a vineyard?

____

2. Explain what you must do to maintain good friendships.

____

3. If you have an array of options from which to choose, will it be easy to make a selection? Explain.

____

4. What type of vegetation would you like to see in a garden? Explain your answer.

____

5. Is the President of the United States a person of renown? Explain.

____

6. Explain what you need to do to help a seed sprout into a plant.

____

7. Is it desirable to cram for a test? Explain your answer.

____

8. If mosquitoes abound during your vacation, what would you do?

____

Name ______________________ Date ______________

***from the* Bible: "The Creation and the Fall"** and **"The Story of the Flood"**

Reading Warm-up A

Read the following passage. Pay special attention to the underlined words. Then, read it again, and complete the activities. Use a separate sheet of paper for your written answers.

Some people believe that the remains of Noah's Ark can be found within the great expanse of Mount Ararat. According to legend, the ark came to rest somewhere within this large area after the floodwaters receded. However, Mount Ararat is popular with hikers for other reasons.

Many hikers welcome the challenge of climbing Mount Ararat despite the mountain's harsh climate. This climate is created in part because of the high altitude. Hikers climbing Mount Ararat on a sunny day can suddenly find themselves in the midst of a terrible storm. Being in the middle of such a storm can be exciting and, dangerous. Second, there is the difficult terrain. Together, the mountain's climate and terrain make exploration as thrilling as it is perilous.

Over the years, people have devised various ways to reach Mount Ararat's summit. Some have hiked to the top, and others have flown around it. Many climbers who started a journey up the mountain have been forced to terminate their trek because of the difficulty and danger involved. Any mountain that comprised such steep, rocky slopes would be attractive to hikers; the attraction of Mount Ararat is increased by its connection to the ancient Biblical story of Noah. Those who have fashioned plans to reach the top of Mount Ararat are encouraged by its mystery and their own eagerness to reach its peak.

1. Underline the phrase that explains what expanse means. Use ***expanse*** in a sentence.

2. Underline the phrase that tells what happened to the ark after the floodwaters receded. What might the ground have looked like after the waters ***receded***?

3. Circle the phrase that tells what created Mount Ararat's harsh climate. Tell what ***created*** means.

4. Underline the phrase that explains what midst means. Use ***midst*** in a sentence.

5. List one way that people have devised to reach the top of Mount Ararat. Then, explain what ***devised*** means.

6. Underline the phrase that explains why hikers have been forced to terminate their journeys up Mount Ararat. Then, use the word ***terminate*** in a sentence.

7. Underline the words that tell what the mountain comprised. Write a sentence of your own using the word ***comprised***.

8. Underline the phrase that tells why people have fashioned plans to reach the top of Mount Ararat. Tell what ***fashioned*** means.

Name ______________________________ Date ______________

***from the* Bible: "The Creation and the Fall"** and **"The Story of the Flood"**

Reading Warm-up B

Read the following passage. Pay special attention to the underlined words. Then, read it again, and complete the activities. Use a separate sheet of paper for your written answers.

Planting a vineyard takes a great deal of hard work and planning. You need to examine your property to determine whether you can successfully maintain grapevines there. Climate, water supply, soil quality, and possibility of disease are all points that must be considered. Any excess vegetation that is growing on the land needs to be removed as well.

You must also select the type of grapes that will grow best on your land. This process is challenging because of the array of grape varieties that will be presented to you in many different categories. Grape varieties of renown may not be the best varieties to plant on your property. Just because you have heard of them does not mean that they will grow well in your soil. Match the grape variety to the soil type to ensure that the grapevines will sprout successfully rather than die on your property.

It is also important to examine the market for grapes in your area. If vineyards abound in the region, competition will be stiff and it will be difficult to make a good profit. It may be worthwhile to specialize in a variety of grape that is not grown by others.

Finally, growing grapes is a large investment in labor and time. It is desirable to save a large amount of money before you plant your grapes in order to meet expenses. You are not likely to make a profit for the first three to five years after you plant the vines, but with hard work, planning, and a little bit of luck, you too may be successful at growing grapes.

1. Circle the words that explain what vineyard means. Use *vineyard* in a sentence.
2. Explain what you must examine to determine whether you can maintain grapevines. Describe something else that a person might *maintain* on his or her property.
3. Underline the phrase that is a clue to the meaning of vegetation. Use *vegetation* in a sentence.
4. Underline the phrase that explains what is in the array. Use *array* in a sentence.
5. Underline the phrase that is a clue to the meaning of renown. Tell what *renown* means.
6. Underline the phrase that tells what sprout means. Use *sprout* in a sentence.
7. Why will competition be stiff if vineyards abound in your area? Tell what *abound* means.
8. Underline the phrase that explains why it is desirable to save money before you plant grapes in a vineyard. Tell what *desirable* means.

Name ______________________ Date ______________

***from the* Bible: Genesis 1–3, "The Creation and the Fall," and 6–9, "The Story of the Flood"**

Literary Analysis: Archetypal Setting

An **archetypal setting** is a time, place, or landscape that has similar significance for many different peoples. Such common settings arise across cultures because they apparently connect to the most powerful or universal human experiences. Here are some common archetypal settings:

- a paradise, or ideal place where people live without strife or fear
- a universe made up of opposites
- a landscape that emerges from dark or watery emptiness or confusion
- a circle that symbolizes completion
- a giant tree that connects heaven and earth
- a great flood and a ship that survives it
- an underworld that people go to after they die

DIRECTIONS: *In the left-hand column of the following chart, list the archetypal settings that appear in these chapters from Genesis. In the right-hand column, list the key information provided about each place.*

Archetypal Setting	Key Details About It

Name ______________________________ Date ______________

from the **Bible: Genesis 1–3, "The Creation and the Fall," and 6–9, "The Story of the Flood"**

Reading Strategy: Identify Chronological Order

The events in the first chapter of Genesis are told in **chronological order,** the order in which they happen in time. Transitional words and phrases, like *first, next, before, on the third day,* and *finally,* help make the chronological order clear.

A. DIRECTIONS: *On the lines, number each sentence to show the correct chronological order of these events from the first chapter of Genesis. Use the context clues to help you.*

____ Then God separated light from darkness, and it was the first day.

____ Last of all came the first human beings.

____ On the third day, God gathered the waters together, let dry land emerge, and covered the land with vegetation.

____ Then, on the seventh day, God rested.

____ Fourth came the sun, moon, and stars to signal day and night.

____ In the beginning, there was a void.

____ God created fish and birds on the fifth day.

____ On the second day, God separated the sky from the water.

B. DIRECTIONS: *Sum up the story of the flood in five sentences, using chronological order.*

____

____

____

____

____

Name ______________________ Date ______________

from the Bible: Genesis 1–3, "The Creation and the Fall," and 6–9, "The Story of the Flood"

Vocabulary Builder

Using the Prefix *com-*

The prefix *com-* means "with" or "together." It occurs in the word *comprised,* which means "went together to form."

A. DIRECTIONS: *Use your knowledge of the prefix* com- *to define each word. Write the definition on the lines. Consult a dictionary if you need help.*

1. comparison: ______________________
2. companion: ______________________
3. compassion: ______________________
4. compatible: ______________________
5. communicate: ______________________

Using the Word List

void	shrewdest	enmity	covenant
expanse	duped	corrupt	comprised

B. DIRECTIONS: *Write the word from the Word List on the line before its definition.*

1. ______________: tricked; fooled
2. ______________: spoiled by sin or dishonesty; rotten
3. ______________: included; made up
4. ______________: total emptiness
5. ______________: very large open area

C. DIRECTIONS: *Write the letter of the word that makes the relationship of the second pair of words closest to the relationship of the pair of words in capital letters.*

___ 1. PROCLAMATION : SPEECH :: covenant :
A. organization B. church C. agreement D. debate

___ 2. HAPPINESS : SMILE :: enmity :
A. fight B. hug C. enemy D. discharge

___ 3. STINGIEST : CHEAP :: shrewdest :
A. dishonest B. clever C. peaceful D. loud

Name ______________________ Date ______________

***from the* Bible: Genesis 1–3, "The Creation and the Fall," and 6–9, "The Story of the Flood"**

Grammar and Style: Punctuation in Dialogue

Dialogue presents a speaker's exact words between opening (") and closing (") quotation marks. In punctuating dialogue, keep these rules in mind:

- A period or a comma always goes inside the closing quotation mark.

  God said, "It is not good for man to be alone**."**

  "I will make a fitting helper for him**,"** God decided.

- A question mark or exclamation point goes inside the closing quotation mark if it is the end punctuation of the quotation itself.

  God called to the man, "Where are you**?"**

- A question mark or exclamation point goes outside the closing quotation mark if it is not the end punctuation of the quotation itself.

  Did God say, "It is not good for man to be alone**"?**

A. Practice: *Rewrite these sentences on the lines provided. Correctly insert any missing punctuation.*

1. When did God say, Let there be light? ______________________

2. Let the earth bring forth every kind of living creature, God said. ______________________

3. After creating Adam and Eve, God told them, Fill the earth and master it. ______________________

4. The serpent asked Eve, Did God really say not to eat of that tree? ______________________

B. Writing Application: *Write five short sentences of a dialogue that Noah might have had in order to persuade a family member to come onto the ark. Include at least one question. Be sure to punctuate your sentences correctly.*

1. ______________________
2. ______________________
3. ______________________
4. ______________________
5. ______________________

Name ______________________________ Date ______________

from the Bible: Genesis 1–3, "The Creation and the Fall," and 6–9, "The Story of the Flood"

Support for Writing

For your extended definition, use the graphic organizer below to help you organize your prewriting and drafting steps: creating a definition of paradise and then expanding it with examples.

Word

paradise

↓

Define

↓

Examples

____

____

____

____

Name ______________________________ Date ______________

from the **Bible: Genesis 1–3, "The Creation and the Fall," and 6–9, "The Story of the Flood"**

Support for Extend Your Learning

Research and Technology

In gathering information for your **written report** on other flood stories in literature, it might be useful for you to keep in mind how those stories are similar to and different from the account of the flood in the Book of Genesis in the Bible. Use the following graphic organizer (or one like it) to help you organize your information (you may find more or fewer examples than the number listed on the chart).

Other Floods in Literature and Mythology	Similarities to Genesis Flood	Differences from Genesis Flood
Flood 1:		
Flood 2:		
Flood 3:		
Flood 4:		

Listening and Speaking

Use the questions and lines below to help you to plan your **choral reading** from Genesis.

1. How many students should there be in the choral reading group? ____________
2. Should the whole group read each section, or should smaller subgroups read each section?
   ____
   ____
3. Should there be any solo passages? Should individuals take on specific roles and read the dialogue as individuals while the whole group reads the narration portions?
   ____
   ____
4. Should the reading slow down or speed up at various points? Get louder or softer?
   ____
   ____
5. How often should we rehearse?
   ____
   ____

Name ______________________ Date ______________

from the **Bible: Genesis 1–3, "The Creation and the Fall," and 6–9, "The Story of the Flood"**

Enrichment: Science

Snakes are members of the reptile family that resemble lizards without limbs. Some snakes are small; some are several feet long. Being limbless, they propel themselves along the ground with startling rapidity through a combination of side-to-side movements and a kind of thrusting of their scaly skin, which is attached to their ribs. The scales also help them retain water. They absorb heat from the environment, as all "cold-blooded" creatures do, instead of generating their own.

Snakes are found in all climates except the polar regions. Some prefer land, some are tree dwellers, and some prefer water, though even water snakes have lungs, not gills, and must come up for air. They are carnivorous, or meat eating, living mainly on small animals, such as rodents, frogs, and insects. Because they have no limbs to hold their prey, snakes swallow their food whole and have special ligaments in their jawbones and skulls that allow them to open wide enough to do so. Many snakes swallow prey alive; some coil around it and crush it to death first; and some have developed poisonous venom to paralyze or kill it. The venom comes out of special teeth, called fangs, located in the snake's top jaw. Only a small number of snakes are poisonous. In North America, these include rattlesnakes, coral snakes, and water moccasins. Rattlesnakes are unusual in that they have horny rings on their tails that make a rattling sound designed to frighten away predators. Snakes do not have larynxes and so cannot cry out, but most can make a hissing sound that can be quite loud.

DIRECTIONS: *Answer these questions based on what you read above and the excerpt from the Bible.*

1. Would the snake who tempted Eve look more like today's snakes or lizards? Explain.

____

____

2. Snakes are not too popular. How might the Bible story contribute to their negative image?

____

____

3. Give at least two physical reasons that may also help explain snakes' unpopularity.

____

____

4. In what ways might snakes be helpful to human beings?

____

____

5. Would you guess that snakes in cold climates might hibernate in winter? Why?

____

____

Name ______________________________ Date ______________

***from the* Bible: Genesis 1–3, "The Creation and the Fall," and 6–9, "The Story of the Flood"**

Selection Test A

Critical Reading *Identify the letter of the choice that best answers the question.*

____ 1. Which element of an archetypal setting is in this passage from Genesis: "God made the expanse, and it separated the water which was below the expanse from the water which was above the expanse"?

A. a big universe

B. a paradise

C. a tree that connects heaven and earth

D. a landscape that comes from water

____ 2. What are the first words of God in Chapter 1 of Genesis that caused day and night?

A. "Let there be light."

B. "Let the water below the sky be gathered."

C. "Be fertile and increase."

D. "Let the earth sprout vegetation."

____ 3. Of all the living things created by God in the beginning of Genesis, when was man created?

A. first, before light

B. second, after light

C. third, before the water

D. last, after other creations

____ 4. Which aspect of an archetypal setting is shown in the Genesis description of the Garden of Eden?

A. a world of opposites

B. a paradise

C. a tree that connects heaven and earth

D. a landscape that comes from water

____ 5. Which word best describes Eve in her dealings with the serpent in Genesis, Chapter 2?

A. sneaky

B. cruel

C. innocent

D. bitter

Name ______________________ Date ______________

____ 6. What is the archetypal setting for Eve's taking and eating the fruit in Genesis, Chapter 3?
A. a world of opposites
B. a paradise
C. a tree that connects heaven and earth
D. a landscape that comes from water

____ 7. In Genesis, Chapter 3, what does God create by saying Adam will use his own "sweat" and toil forever?
A. human intelligence
B. human creativity
C. human wealth
D. human suffering

____ 8. Which emotion best describes God's reaction to human evil in Genesis, Chapter 6?
A. anger
B. kindness
C. amusement
D. fear

____ 9. In Chapters 6–9 of Genesis, which word best describes Noah's personality?
A. obedient
B. lazy
C. fearful
D. bossy

____ 10. In Genesis, Chapter 9, how does God make sure that humans will continue to be obedient?
A. God threatens humans with more floods.
B. God sets up a covenant with humans.
C. God says that humans will never work again.
D. God makes all humans kind and good.

____ 11. Which archetypal setting is shown when the Great Flood ends in Chapters 6–9 of Genesis?
A. a world of opposites
B. a paradise
C. a tree that connects heaven and earth
D. a landscape that comes from water

Name ______________________ Date ____________

Vocabulary and Grammar

___ 12. According to the Book of Genesis, what existed before the creation of the world?
- A. an expanse
- B. a covenant
- C. a void
- D. enmity

___ 13. Which of the following words is closest in meaning to *covenant*?
- A. creation
- B. contract
- C. temptation
- D. flood

___ 14. Which sentence is punctuated correctly?
- A. The teacher asked. "How many of you have read the Book of Genesis"?
- B. The teacher asked, "How many of you have read the Book of Genesis?"
- C. The teacher, asked "How many of you have read the Book of Genesis"?
- D. The teacher, asked "How many of you have read the Book of Genesis?"

___ 15. What change is needed to punctuate this sentence correctly?

Was it before or after the Flood that Noah said to Ham, "Cursed be Canaan?"
- A. Remove the comma after *Ham*.
- B. Move the question mark outside the end quotation mark.
- C. Add a comma after *Noah*.
- D. Replace the question mark with a period.

Essay

16. According to Genesis, is the serpent or Eve more to blame for Eve's eating the fruit of the tree of knowledge? Explain your view in an essay. Support your opinion with reasoning and examples.

17. How does God's attitude toward human weakness change during the story of Noah and the Flood (Genesis, Chapters 6–9)? Develop your views in an essay supported by examples from the text.

Name ________________________________ Date ____________________

from the Bible: Genesis 1–3, "The Creation and the Fall," and 6–9, "The Story of the Flood"

Selection Test B

Critical Reading *Identify the letter of the choice that best completes the statement or answers the question.*

____ 1. Which of these archetypal settings is best illustrated in the opening paragraph of Genesis?
- A. a plant that connects heaven and earth
- B. a starless night
- C. a great sea that cleanses the human spirit
- D. a universe of opposites

____ 2. What are God's first words in the Creation?
- A. "Let there be light."
- B. "Let there be an expanse in the midst of the water."
- C. He called the light Day, and the darkness he called Night.
- D. "Be fertile and increase."

____ 3. Of the following living things, which does God create first?
- A. sea monsters
- B. birds
- C. trees
- D. insects

____ 4. Which detail most clearly stresses humanity's special place among living things?
- A. God creates Adam from earth's dust.
- B. God creates Eve to keep Adam company.
- C. God creates Adam in God's image.
- D. God creates Eve from Adam's rib.

____ 5. Which phrase best describes the Garden of Eden?
- A. a lush paradise
- B. a barren wasteland
- C. a farm with several crops
- D. an overgrown jungle

____ 6. Which phrase best describes Adam and Eve in the Garden of Eden?
- A. selfish and greedy
- B. innocent and gullible
- C. hard-working and obedient
- D. frivolous and wasteful

____ 7. What does the serpent most clearly seem to represent?
- A. human hunger for knowledge
- B. the animal kingdom
- C. temptation to evil
- D. Eve's conscience

Name ______________________ Date ______________

____ 8. Which of the following do the stories of the Creation and the Garden of Eden *not* help to explain?
A. the origin of human suffering
B. the origin of resting on the Sabbath
C. the reason snakes have no limbs
D. the reason God created the Earth

____ 9. Why does God cause the Flood?
A. to end a terrible drought
B. to reward Noah and his family
C. to reduce the population
D. to punish humanity for its sins

____ 10. Which word best describes the kind of person Noah is?
A. virtuous
B. bossy
C. gullible
D. unskilled

____ 11. Which of these archetypal settings is central to "The Story of the Flood"?
A. a garden paradise
B. a boat on which life survives
C. a river crossed when a person dies
D. a sea that parts miraculously

____ 12. In "The Story of the Flood," which of these events happens first?
A. Noah sends out a raven that cannot find a place to land.
B. Noah sends out a dove that comes back with an olive leaf.
C. The ark comes to rest on the mountains of Ararat.
D. The rain stops but the waters continue to swell for some time.

____ 13. Which characteristic does God most clearly display in Chapters 1–3 and 6–9 of Genesis?
A. mercy
B. power
C. an air of mystery
D. a sense of humor

____ 14. What sort of detail does the Bible typically provide to help pinpoint events chronologically?
A. It describes changes to places, such as Eden and Mount Ararat, over time.
B. It states the year according to the lunar calendar of the Jewish religion.
C. At the start of each chapter, it indicates how many days have passed since the creation.
D. It lists generations of descendants in the families of the characters in the Bible.

____ 15. Which of these archetypal settings is *not* clearly illustrated in Chapters 1–3 and 6–9 of Genesis?
A. an ideal place
B. a landscape that emerges from watery chaos
C. a communal hall where people congregate
D. a universe comprised of opposites

Name ______________________________ Date ______________

Vocabulary and Grammar

____ 16. Which word best describes the serpent in the Garden of Eden?
A. void
B. comprised
C. shrewd
D. duped

____ 17. The Bible says that after the incident in Eden, women and serpents will have *enmity* between them. What does that statement suggest?
A. Women and snakes will be hostile to each other.
B. Women will recognize the value of snakes in the cycle of nature.
C. Women and snakes will never again have contact.
D. In general, women will be more forgiving than men.

____ 18. What *covenant* is made in Chapters 1–3 or 6–9 of Genesis?
A. God orders Adam and Eve not to eat from the tree of knowledge.
B. The serpent tricks Eve into disobeying God's command.
C. Eve persuades Adam to join her in disobeying God's command.
D. God promises Noah that he will never again destroy all of humanity.

____ 19. What changes, if any, would you make to this sentence?
God said "Did you eat of the tree from which I had forbidden you to eat?"
A. Add a comma after *said.*
B. Eliminate the quotation marks.
C. Place the question mark after the closing quotation mark.
D. The sentence is correct as it is.

____ 20. Which sentence is correctly punctuated?
A. He said to the woman, "Did God really say you shall not eat of any tree in the garden"?
B. The woman replied to the serpent, "We may eat of the fruit of the other trees".
C. The Lord God called out to the man and said to him, "Where are you?"
D. God said to the woman, "What is this you have done"!

Essay

21. Write a short essay describing of the Garden of Eden. Explain what it looks like and why it is a paradise, or ideal place. Base the essay on your reading of Genesis.

22. Write an essay about the relationship between God and human beings in Chapters 1–3 and 6–9 of Genesis. Discuss the benefits or rewards that human beings receive from God and the reasons God punishes Adam, Eve, and other human beings.

23. Discuss at least four different practices or aspects of human experience that Chapters 1–3 and 6–9 of Genesis help to explain. You might begin with the creation itself.

Vocabulary Warm-up Word Lists

Study these words from the selections. Then, complete the activities.

Word List A

abiding [uh BYD ing] *adj.* long-lasting
John has had an abiding dislike of carrots since childhood.

adorned [uh DAWRND] *v.* decorated with
The queen's hands were adorned with many large rings.

inflicted [in FLIKT id] *v.* caused harm or pain by forceful action
The bee inflicted great pain by stinging Jane's arm.

molest [muh LEST] *v.* disturb; annoy
The kittens are sleeping, so do not molest their peace.

morsel [MAWR suhl] *n.* a small piece or amount
No cake was left because the children had eaten every morsel of it.

prosper [PRAHS per] *v.* thrive; make steady progress
You will prosper in your career if you work hard.

splendor [SPLEN der] *n.* something magnificent; brilliance
We enjoyed watching the splendor of the tropical sunset.

steadfast [STED fast] *adj.* constant; loyal
My dog is my steadfast companion.

Word List B

deceased [dee SEEST] *adj.* no longer living; dead
We learned that Mr. Brown was deceased when we read his obituary.

dominate [DAHM i nayt] *v.* control by superior power or authority
Sarah is able to dominate the soccer field because of her speed.

formerly [FAWR mer lee] *adv.* at an earlier time; once
Before marriage, Bev Smith was formerly known as Bev Johnson.

handiwork [HAN dee werk] *n.* anything made by a particular person
That quilt is just one example of my grandmother's handiwork.

interference [in ter FEER uhns] *n.* act that gets in the way or prevents
Crowd interference kept the police from reaching the crime scene.

perpetuated [per PECH oo ay tid] *v.* prolonged; continued
Michael perpetuated the tension by arguing with his co-workers.

sustain [suh STAYN] *v.* to keep up; to support
Jim could not sustain the fast pace of the race, so he dropped out.

withheld [with HELD] *v.* refrained from giving; did not grant
I withheld my answer to the invitation until I heard who else was going.

Name ______________________________ Date ______________

from the **Bible: The Book of Ruth** and **Psalms 8, 19, 23, and 137**

Vocabulary Warm-up Exercises

Exercise A *Fill in each blank below with the appropriate word from Word List A.*

We couldn't believe the [1] ________________ of the treasures on display at the museum. One statue was [2] ________________ with a crown that contained over two hundred jewels. The museum guide told us that the crown once belonged to a terrible king who [3] ________________ great suffering on his people because of his desire for jewels. As a result of the king's greed, the people failed to [4] ________________. At one point, it was said that the king refused to provide even a [5] ________________ of food to his people unless they brought him more riches. The people in the kingdom developed an [6] ________________ dislike for their selfish ruler. They began to [7] ________________ the royal officers by throwing stones at them when they came to collect taxes. Their opposition to the king was [8] ________________, not changing or wavering, and eventually they overthrew him.

Exercise B *Answer the questions with complete explanations.*

1. What might a kindergarten student do with the handiwork that he or she created in class?

   ____

2. Where might you look for information about someone who is deceased?

   ____

3. Explain what your opponents might think of you if you dominate in a sport.

   ____

4. If you withheld your judgment about something, did you express your opinion about it? Explain.

   ____

5. Was every bird formerly an egg? Explain.

   ____

6. If someone perpetuated a rumor about your best friend, what would you do about it?

   ____

7. Explain what you must do to sustain good grades in school.

   ____

8. If you were experiencing radio interference, what might you hear?

   ____

Name ______________________________ Date ______________

from the **Bible: The Book of Ruth** and **Psalms 8, 19, 23, and 137**

Reading Warm-up A

Read the following passage. Pay special attention to the underlined words. Then, read it again, and complete the activities. Use a separate sheet of paper for your written answers.

Growing up in Cuba, Ana lived a life of splendor and luxury. She wore fancy dresses that were adorned with silk ribbons and embroidery. She lived in a large mansion in a well-to-do neighborhood in Havana, and she took trips to exotic places with her family. She ate fine food, and she had servants who attended her every wish. In short, Ana had a very privileged life.

When the revolution occurred, Ana's life changed dramatically. She and her family were forced to leave Cuba, so they came to the United States for greater security and protection. However, their new life was difficult because Ana's family had to leave their wealth behind. Her parents could not find enough steady employment to prosper, and soon the money they had began running out. They could barely afford what they needed. In Cuba, dinner was an extravagant affair. The delicious dishes were often left unfinished. Now, not a single morsel of food was wasted.

School in the United States was challenging for Ana. The other students were not kind, and they inflicted a cruel form of punishment on her because she did not fit in. They teased her about the way she spoke, the way she dressed, and her refined manner. It was nearly impossible for Ana to speak out against these attacks.

Ana was not completely alone, though. Amy, a considerate girl at school, noticed how Ana suffered when the other children would molest her with their merciless insults. Amy had an abiding dislike for such behavior. From the time she was a small child, she was an enemy of bullies. Whenever she saw Ana being teased, Amy would come to her defense. The other children eventually stopped bothering Ana.

Of course, Ana was grateful for Amy's help. In return, Amy respected Ana for her strength in enduring such difficulties, and the two girls became steadfast friends, always loyal and faithful to each other.

1. Underline the word that is a clue to the meaning of splendor. Give your own example of ***splendor***.
2. Circle the words that explain what adorned the dresses. Use ***adorned*** in a sentence.
3. Circle the words that show the opposite of what it means to prosper. Why would a person want to ***prosper*** in life?
4. Underline the phrase that explains why Ana and her family could not waste a morsel of food. Then, tell what ***morsel*** means.
5. Underline the words that are a clue to the meaning of inflicted. Then, explain why the students probably ***inflicted*** cruelty on Ana.
6. Circle the word that tells how Ana felt when the children would molest her with their insults. Tell what ***molest*** means.
7. Circle the phrase that shows that Amy's dislike is abiding. Then, tell what ***abiding*** means.
8. Underline the phrase that is a clue to the meaning of steadfast. Then, tell what ***steadfast*** means.

Name ______________________________ Date ______________

from the **Bible: The Book of Ruth** and **Psalms 8, 19, 23, and 137**

Reading Warm-up B

Read the following passage. Pay special attention to the underlined words. Then, read it again, and complete the activities. Use a separate sheet of paper for your written answers.

The land formerly known as Moab is found today within the boundaries of present-day Jordan. Moab's territory consisted of three parts. First, there was the Field of Moab, which was protected on three sides by the gorge of the Arnon River in the north, by the Dead Sea cliffs in the west, and by a circle of hills in the east. Second, the Land of Moab was made up of wide-open country from the Arnon River north to the hills of Gilead. Third, the Plains of Moab was a lush and fertile area in the low, tropical valleys of the Jordan river.

Many stories about Moab have been perpetuated through scripture in the Bible. When the Israelites were freed from Egypt, they approached Moab, seeking passage to Palestine, but the Moabites refused. However, Moab did not fight Israel. Instead, the two societies lived as peaceful neighbors for over 300 years. Moab no longer exists, and the Moabites have died out as a people. However, recent explorations of the area have revealed new information about the long-deceased people who lived there.

The Moabites were able to sustain themselves by growing their own food and raising sheep in the fertile valleys. They were also able to dominate the region in wool production, as the recent discovery of a loom helps show. It is believed that other peoples in the area bought their wool from the Moabites.

Scientists learned about the Moabites' handiwork with wool by reading an ancient stone tablet called the Mesha inscription. The tablet also tells other stories about Moab—takes that history had withheld until the discovery of the stone brought the stories to light. From this tablet, scientists have learned that the Moabites were closely related to the people of Israel in both language and thought. Although the Moabites were a peaceful people, the interference of invaders brought an end to their independence and they were absorbed into other empires.

1. Circle the word that means the opposite of formerly. Then, use *formerly* in a sentence of your own.
2. Underline the phrase that tells where the stories about Moab were perpetuated. Name another way in which a story can be *perpetuated*.
3. Underline the phrase that is a clue to the meaning of deceased. Use *deceased* in a sentence.
4. Explain what the Moabites did to sustain themselves. Give an example of what modern people do to *sustain* themselves.
5. In what area of agriculture did the Moabites dominate? Use *dominate* in a sentence.
6. Name two types of handiwork. Explain what *handiwork* means.
7. Underline the phrase that means close to the opposite of withheld. Use *withheld* in a sentence.
8. Circle the words that explain the result of interference. Use *interference* in a sentence.

Name ______________________________ Date ______________

from the **Bible: The Book of Ruth and Psalms 8, 19, 23, and 137**

Literary Analysis: Parallelism

The verses or lines of the Bible often use **parallelism,** in which an idea stated in the first half is repeated, negated, completed, expanded, or otherwise elaborated on in the second half. Parallelism makes verses more powerful and more memorable, and it emphasizes important themes or ideas. Here are some examples of parallelism from the Book of Ruth and the Psalms:

- idea repeated: There is no utterance, there are no words. . . . (Psalms 19:4)
- idea negated: "I went away full, and the LORD brought me back empty." (Ruth 1:21)
- idea completed: "wherever you go, I will go." (Ruth 1:16)
- idea expanded or elaborated on: the birds of the heavens, the fish of the sea (Psalm 8:9)

DIRECTIONS: *Fill in the chart with examples of parallelism from the Book of Ruth or Psalms 8, 19, 23, or 137. Include at least one example of each function.*

Function	Example	Location
1. repeats an idea		
2. negates an idea		
3. completes an idea		
4. expands or elaborates on an idea		

Name ______________________ Date ______________

from the **Bible: The Book of Ruth and Psalms 8, 19, 23, and 137**

Reading Strategy: Use Context Clues

As you read, one of the best ways to figure out the meaning of unfamiliar words is to **use context clues,** or hints in the surrounding text. Common context clues include synonyms and longer restatements, antonyms and other contrasts, and examples that clarify meaning.

In the Book of Ruth, we read that when Ruth met her powerful relative Boaz,

> she *prostrated* herself with her face to the ground.

The word *prostrated* may be unfamiliar, but details in the sentence tell what *prostrating* is. They tell us that Ruth had "her face to the ground." So *prostrated* must mean "to put your face to the ground" or "to lie facedown."

DIRECTIONS: *Use the context clues in these sentences to figure out the meaning of each word in italics. Write the probable meaning on the lines. Circle the context clues that helped you.*

1. "'Even if I were married tonight and I also bore sons, should you wait for them to grow up? Should you on their account *debar* yourselves from marriage?'" —Ruth 1:12–13

   debar: ______________________

2. "'May the LORD reward your deeds. May you have a full *recompense* from the LORD.'" —Ruth 2:12

   recompense: ______________________

3. "At mealtime, Boaz said to her, 'Come over here and *partake* of the meal, and dip your morsel in the vinegar.'" —Ruth 2:14

   partake: ______________________

4. "'I am also acquiring Ruth the Moabite, the wife of Mahlon, as my wife, so as to *perpetuate* the name of the deceased upon his estate, that the name of the deceased may not disappear from among his kinsmen and from the gate of his home town.'" —Ruth 4:10

   perpetuate: ______________________

5. "Day to day makes *utterance,* / night to night speaks out." —Psalm 19:3

   utterance: ______________________

6. "You *anoint* my head with oil. . . ." —Psalm 23:5

   anoint: ______________________

7. "If I forget you, O Jerusalem, / let my right hand wither; / let my tongue stick to my *palate*. . . ." —Psalm 137:5–6

   palate: ______________________

Name ______________________________ Date ______________

from the **Bible: The Book of Ruth and Psalms 8, 19, 23, and 137**

Vocabulary Builder

Using the Anglo-Saxon Root *-stead-*

The Anglo-Saxon root *-stead-* means "place." The word *steadfast* combines that root with the word *fast* in the sense of "staying the same" (like *fast* colors, which do not run). *Steadfast* means "staying in the same place" or "enduring."

A. Directions: *On the lines, explain how the meaning of the root* -stead- *is part of the meaning of the following words.*

1. instead: ______________________________
2. farmstead: ______________________________
3. bedstead: ______________________________
4. steady: ______________________________

Using the Word List

glean	redeem	avenger	lucid
reapers	precepts	steadfast	

B. Directions: *Answer each question with a word from the Word List.*

1. Who is probably motivated by a desire to get even? ______________
2. What are moral persons likely to follow? ______________
3. What might you do to find grain in a field? ______________
4. What might you do to free a captive? ______________
5. How would you describe an argument that makes perfect sense? ______________
6. How would you describe someone who is always loyal? ______________
7. What would you call those who gather grain in a field? ______________

C. Directions: *Write the letter of the word that means the opposite or nearly the opposite of the Word List word.*

____	1. reapers	A. harvesters	B. planters	C. farmers	D. customers
____	2. lucid	A. obscure	B. light	C. weighty	D. muscular
____	3. steadfast	A. hungry	B. satisfied	C. unrewarding	D. unreliable

Name ______________________________ Date ______________

from the **Bible: The Book of Ruth and Psalms 8, 19, 23, and 137**

Grammar and Style: Compound Predicates

The **predicate** is the part of a sentence that tells what the subject does or is. In a **compound predicate,** two or more verbs that have the same subject are joined by a conjunction such as *and, but,* or *or.* In all three of the following sentences, the subject is *Ruth;* the main verbs are in italics.

Ruth *loved* and *supported* her mother-in-law, Naomi.

Ruth *was born* a Moabite but *chose* to become an Israelite.

Ruth *joined* Naomi, *traveled* to Naomi's home, and *gleaned* barley in the fields.

A. Practice: *For each sentence below, underline the subject once, circle the conjunction that joins the parts of the compound predicate, and underline twice the verbs that make up that compound predicate.*

1. During a famine, Naomi's family came to the land of the Moabites and remained there.
2. Naomi lost her husband and was left with two sons.
3. Both of Naomi's sons married Moabites but then died too.
4. The daughters-in-law could remain with the Moabites or go with Naomi back to Judah.
5. Orpah, unlike Ruth, stayed with her people and did not accompany Naomi.

B. Writing Application: *Write five sentences about Ruth's experiences in Judah. Use a compound predicate in each sentence. Underline twice the verbs that make up the compound predicate, underline their subject once, and circle the conjunction that joins them.*

1. ______________________________
____
2. ______________________________
____
3. ______________________________
____
4. ______________________________
____
5. ______________________________
____

Name ______________________ Date ______________

from the **Bible: The Book of Ruth and Psalms 8, 19, 23, and 137**

Support for Writing

Use the chart below to help you identify the element of the Book of Ruth that affected you most strongly, summarize your reaction to that element, and find details in the work that support and clarify your reaction. Then, write a thesis statement that clearly states your reaction and the reasons for it.

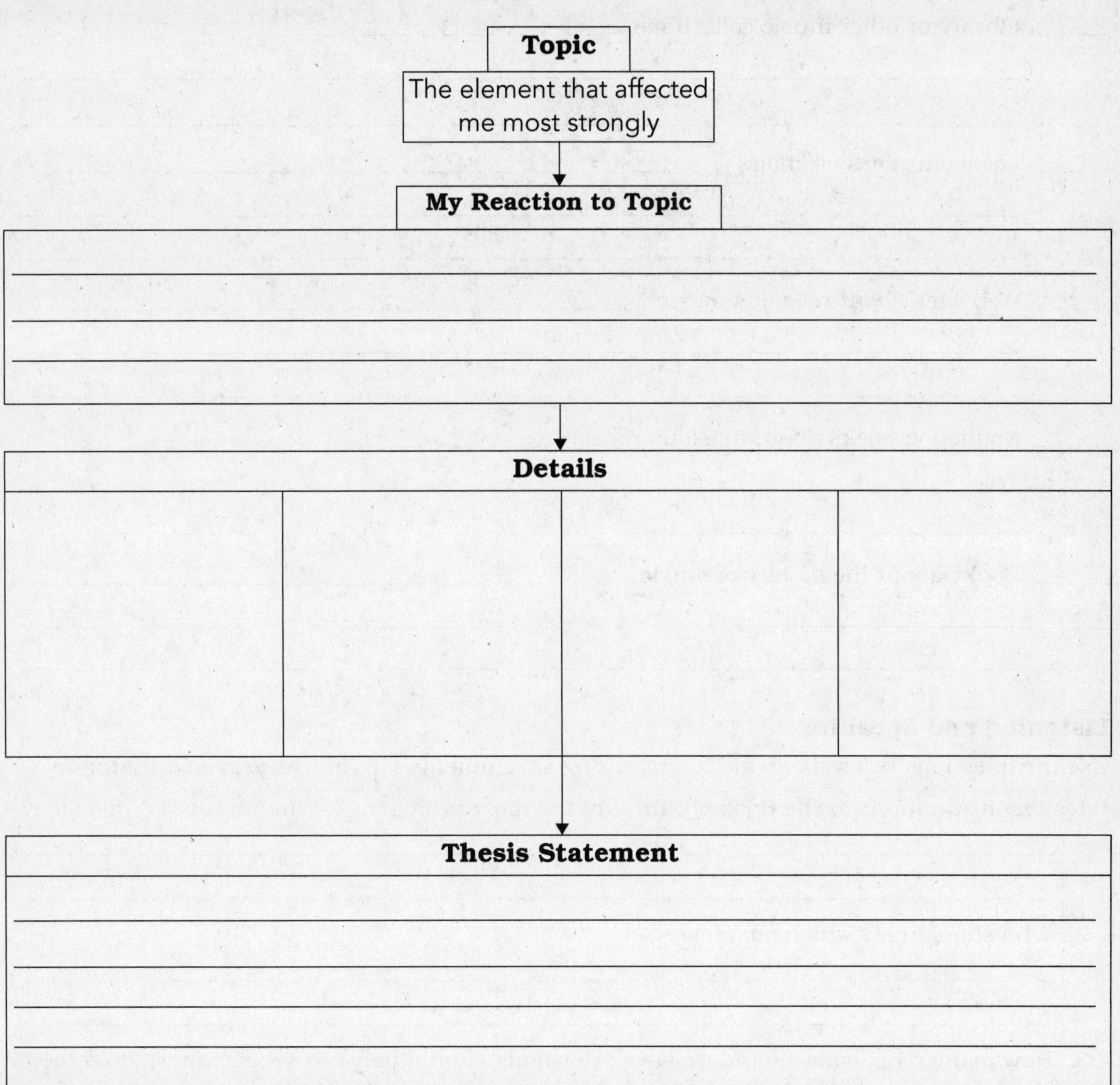

Now, use your notes to help you finish the drafting stage of your essay.

Name ______________________________ Date ______________

from the **Bible: The Book of Ruth and Psalms 8, 19, 23, and 137**

Support for Extend Your Learning

Research and Technology

Use the checklist below to help you organize your search for sources for your **multimedia report** on musical settings of the Psalms. Use the blank space after each item to note the materials you were able to find in that category.

_____ Library or other music collections ______________________________

_____ Local churches or choirs ______________________________

_____ Web sites about religious music ______________________________

_____ Nonfiction books about religious music ______________________________

_____ Books about the history of music ______________________________

Listening and Speaking

Use the questions below as an aid in organizing assignments for your **improvised dialogue.**

1. Which situations in the Book of Ruth are the most promising for an improvised dialogue?

____

2. Who should play which characters?

____

3. How many rehearsals should we have? How long should they be? When can we hold them?

____

Name ______________________ Date ______________

from the **Bible: The Book of Ruth and Psalms 8, 19, 23, and 137**

Enrichment: Marriage Laws and Practices

Ruth weds Boaz according to the Jewish laws of their time, which governed marriage in their community. These laws specified that on the death of a woman's husband the dead husband's closest male relative should take responsibility for the widow by marrying her. Because th kinsman most closely related to Ruth's deceased husband cannot afford to take on the responsibility of marrying Ruth, Boaz, the next closest kinsman, takes over that responsibility.

DIRECTIONS: *Do library or Internet research to find information about marriage laws and customs that can help you answer these questions. Circle the letter of the correct choice.*

1. Which body or bodies establish most of the requirements for legal marriages in the United States?
   - A. the federal government
   - B. state governments
   - C. religious organizations
   - D. the United Nations
2. In order to get married in the United States, which of the following do you need?
   - A. a passport
   - B. a high-school diploma
   - C. a marriage license
   - D. all of the above
3. Which is the most accurate statement about marriage laws in the United States?
   - A. Most places require a physical exam before marriage.
   - B. Some places require blood tests before marriage.
   - C. In most places, people must be twenty-one to marry without parental consent.
   - D. In most places, no one under eighteen can marry, even with parental consent.
4. Which of the following is illegal throughout the United States?
   - A. bigamy
   - B. proxy marriages
   - C. military weddings
   - D. all of the above
5. In the United States, which of the following officials may solemnize a marriage?
   - A. a justice of the peace
   - B. a tribal judge
   - C. a clergyman
   - D. all of the above
6. What are *banns*?
   - A. church proclamations of an intended marriage
   - B. church rules guiding who can and cannot marry
   - C. marriage ceremonies performed in a church or another house of worship
   - D. special musicians who play at wedding ceremonies
7. Where can you find the marriage ceremony of the Anglican or Episcopal Church?
   - A. in the Book of Ruth
   - B. in the Book of Mormon
   - C. in the Book of Common Prayer
   - D. in the Magna Carta
8. In which faith are marriages traditionally performed under a canopy called a *chupah*?
   - A. Roman Catholic
   - B. Jewish
   - C. Islamic
   - D. Buddhist
9. In which of these faiths do brides traditionally wear red as a symbol of happiness?
   - A. Greek Orthodox
   - B. Baptist
   - C. Hindu
   - D. Quaker

Name ______________________________ Date ________________

from the **Bible: The Book of Ruth** and **Psalms 8, 19, 23,** and **137**

Selection Test A

Critical Reading *Identify the letter of the choice that best answers the question.*

____ 1. Which word best describes the character of Ruth?
A. unkind
B. angry
C. loyal
D. shy

____ 2. In the Book of Ruth, a *famine* causes Ruth to return to Judah to find something to eat. Given this context, which of the following definitions would fit the word *famine*?
A. an outbreak of disease
B. plenty of food
C. great wealth
D. lack of food

____ 3. When Naomi urges her daughters-in-law to leave her, they weep. Why?
A. They love Naomi and do not want to go.
B. They hate her and want to go home.
C. They need her in order to avoid hunger.
D. They consider her a burden.

____ 4. In the Book of Ruth, what kind of literary technique is used in this quotation: "For wherever you go, I will go; wherever you lodge, I will lodge . . ."?
A. short sentence
B. repetition
C. rhyming
D. description

____ 5. In the Book of Ruth, Naomi is bitter about her *misfortune.* Given this context, which of the following words is closest in meaning to *misfortune*?
A. happiness
B. hardship
C. money
D. wisdom

____ 6. In the Book of Ruth, why is Boaz so grateful to Ruth for her kindness?
A. He has a fatal disease.
B. He is very poor.
C. He is unattractive.
D. He is an old man.

Name ______________________ Date ______________

___ 7. Which of the following would be the best substitute title for the Book of Ruth?
A. The Milk of Human Kindness
B. Looking Out for Number One
C. Happiness Is Owning Land
D. Family Arguments

___ 8. The author of Psalm 8 mentions the moon and stars that God has "set in place." How does the author feel as he or she is writing this psalm?
A. bitter
B. angry
C. grateful
D. hopeless

___ 9. Which pair of phrases from this line of Psalm 19 shows parallelism?
The heavens declare the glory of God, the sky proclaims His handiwork.
A. glory of God . . . sky proclaims
B. heavens declare . . . his handiwork
C. The heavens . . . proclaims His
D. heavens declare . . . sky proclaims

___ 10. In this line from Psalm 23, which word or phrase best helps you understand what *repose* means?
He makes me lie down . . . He leads me to water in places of repose.
A. lie down
B. water
C. places
D. leads me

___ 11. What does the writer of Psalm 137 feel when writing that ". . . we . . . wept, as we thought of Zion," the homeland?
A. forgiveness
B. anger
C. homesickness
D. freedom

___ 12. Why does the psalmist cry out: ". . . a blessing on him who repays you in kind what you have inflicted on us . . ." in Psalm 137?
A. The psalm writer seeks forgiveness.
B. The psalm writer wants revenge.
C. The psalm writer feels homesick.
D. The psalm writer wins freedom.

Name ______________________________ Date ______________

Vocabulary and Grammar

____ 13. Which word is closest in meaning to *lucid*?
A. confusing
B. asleep
C. clear
D. nervous

____ 14. Which word is most nearly **opposite** in meaning to *steadfast*?
A. steady
B. changeable
C. slow
D. clumsy

____ 15. Which sentence contains a compound predicate?
A. Boaz ate and drank and went to lie down.
B. They married women named Orpah and Ruth.
C. The Lord is my shepherd; I lack nothing.
D. May my words and my prayer be acceptable.

Essay

16. In an essay, discuss the role that loyalty plays in the Book of Ruth. Explain whether loyalty is seen as a good or bad quality. Support your explanation with examples from the text.

17. In an essay, discuss the character of Ruth in the Book of Ruth. How does she change, or remain the same, throughout the story? Support your answer with examples.

Name ______________________________ Date ______________

from the **Bible: The Book of Ruth** and **Psalms 8, 19, 23,** and **237**

Selection Test B

Critical Reading *Identify the letter of the choice that best completes the question.*

____ 1. Which event helps prompt Naomi to return from Moab to Judah?
- A. a famine among the Moabites
- B. the marriage of her sons
- C. the death of her sons
- D. the news that Judah is in trouble

____ 2. In which of these remarks from the first chapter of the Book of Ruth does the parallelism involve a contrast or opposition?
- A. May the Lord deal kindly with you, as you have dealt with the dead and with me!
- B. Do not urge me to leave you, to turn back and not follow you.
- C. Call me Mara, for Shaddai has made my lot very bitter.
- D. I went away full, and the Lord has brought me back empty.

____ 3. What is the effect of the parallelism in this remark that Ruth makes to Naomi?

For wherever you go, I will go; wherever you lodge, I will lodge; your people will be my people, and your God my God. [Ruth 1:16]

- A. It provides strong contrasts that show how torn Naomi is about leaving her people.
- B. It completes the idea in the first clause by clarifying where Ruth plans to live.
- C. It helps stress Ruth's commitment to the family and culture into which she has married.
- D. It helps stress the terrible sacrifice Ruth is making by accompanying Naomi.

____ 4. Which character trait does Naomi display when she suggests changing her name to Mara?
- A. courage
- B. creativity
- C. disloyalty
- D. self-pity

____ 5. When Boaz meets Ruth, he recognizes her sacrifice and loyalty to Naomi and says to her,

May the Lord reward your deeds. May you have a full recompense from the Lord, the God of Israel, under whose wings you have sought refuge!

Which word in the passage gives the strongest clue of what *recompense* means?
- A. reward
- B. deeds
- C. full
- D. refuge

____ 6. How does Boaz react when Ruth lies down on the threshing floor?
- A. He is annoyed that she tries to entrap him in marriage.
- B. He is confused by her actions.
- C. He is not surprised because he knows that she loves him and hopes to wed him.
- D. He admires her even more because she is willing to wed an older man in compliance with Naomi's wishes.

Name ______________________________ Date ______________

____ 7. Which of these is an important lesson of the Book of Ruth?
A. Gratitude results from a bountiful harvest.
B. Faithfulness will be rewarded.
C. Strangers should always be trusted.
D. Loyalty knows no bounds.

____ 8. Why is it significant that Ruth the Moabite is the ancestor of King David?
A. It shows that even a king may have some dubious ancestry.
B. It shows that foreigners can make important contributions to a society.
C. It shows that Ruth had royal blood all along.
D. It shows that a marriage of convenience can turn into one of love.

____ 9. Based on the psalms you have read, what would you say is the chief purpose of the psalms?
A. to praise God
B. to record landmark events in the history of the Jews
C. to mourn the Babylonian captivity
D. to express romantic love

____ 10. In this verse from Psalm 19, what does the context suggest that *utterance* means?

Day to day makes utterance,
night to night speaks out.
There is no utterance,
there are no words,
whose sound goes unheard.

A. totality
B. daylight
C. speech
D. confusion

____ 11. What is the effect of the parallelism in this verse from Psalm 19?

The precepts of the Lord are just, rejoicing the heart;
the instruction of the Lord is lucid, making the eyes light up.

A. It creates a contrast that shows the joys and dangers of God's love.
B. It elaborates on the kinds of just precepts that the Lord establishes.
C. It emphasizes the value of the Lord's teachings.
D. It completes the idea of the Lord rejoicing the human heart.

____ 12. In this verse from Psalm 23, which phrase gives the best clue to what *repose* means?

He makes me lie down in green pastures;
He leads me to water in places of repose.

A. makes me
B. lie down
C. green pastures
D. to water

Name ______________________________ Date ______________________________

____ 13. How is Psalm 137 different from the other Psalms?
A. It is more poetic.
B. It is sadder and angrier.
C. It celebrates with more wonderful joy.
D. It is more whimsical and witty.

Vocabulary and Grammar

____ 14. What does Ruth do when she *gleans* in Boaz's fields?
A. helps dig up weeds
B. shines
C. gathers grain left over by the reapers
D. listens to gossip and passes it along

____ 15. Which word contains an Anglo-Saxon root that means "place"?
A. avenger
B. lucid
C. precept
D. steadfast

____ 16. Which sentence contains a compound predicate?
A. A man of Bethlehem in Judah, with his wife and two sons, went to reside in the country of Moab.
B. The woman was left without her two sons and without her husband.
C. He handed her roasted grain, and she ate her fill.
D. Then she went over stealthily and uncovered his feet and lay down.

____ 17. What are the verbs in the compound predicate of this sentence?

Meanwhile, Boaz had gone to the gate and sat down there.

A. *had* and *sat down*
B. *gone* and *sat*
C. *had gone* and *sat*
D. *had gone* and *sat down there*

Essay

18. Write a short essay in which you examine what the details in The Book of Ruth reveal about the kind of person Ruth is. Discuss her character traits, attitudes, and behavior, as well as the possible motives for her behavior.

19. Some people have called the Book of Ruth the world's first realistic short story. Do you agree? Write your ideas in an essay that discusses how the selection utilizes story form and whether or not the characterization, setting, and other details seem realistic.

20. Write a short essay about the parallelism in the Psalms. Use examples to show how the use of parallelism makes the Psalms more effective and memorable.

Vocabulary Warm-up Word Lists

Study these words from the selections. Then, complete the activities.

Word List A

affliction [uh FLIK shuhn] *n.* illness; pain or suffering
Gus asked the doctor to treat his mysterious affliction.

charity [CHAR i tee] *n.* help or relief for the poor
Pat exhibits charity when she volunteers at the homeless shelter.

compassionate [kuhm PASH uh nit] *adj.* sympathetic; feeling pity
Compassionate doctors provide sympathy as well as medical attention.

endeavors [en DEV ers] *n.* serious efforts toward a goal
Jack hopes that his endeavors will lead to a career in music.

guidance [GYD uhns] *n.* advice; counsel
I asked my mother for guidance about buying a new car.

relieved [ri LEEVD] *v.* freed from something, such as a duty or pain
Passing the test relieved me of my anxiety.

renown [ri NOWN] *n.* fame
The singer has many fans, giving him worldwide renown.

resume [ri ZOOM] *v.* begin again after an interruption
We will resume baseball practice after the rain stops.

Word List B

abhor [ab HAWR] *v.* view with hatred or revulsion
I abhor broccoli because it tastes foul to me.

astray [uh STRAY] *adv.* away from the correct path or direction
We went astray because we made a wrong turn at the intersection.

created [kree AY tid] *v.* produced; brought into being
The chef created a delicious soup from fresh vegetables.

gratified [GRAT i fyd] *adj.* pleased; satisfied
Janet was gratified by her success at this year's film festival.

incurred [in KERD] *v.* took on or was given something unpleasant
The team incurred a penalty for violating the game's rules.

judgment [JUJ ment] *n.* opinion; ruling
You should not make a judgment about Mark before you meet him.

merciful [MER si fuhl] *adj.* full of sympathy and kindness for others
The merciful king provided food to the starving soldiers.

varied [VER eed] *adj.* different
The students' varied answers to the question surprised their teacher.

Name ______________________________ Date ______________

from the **Qur'an: "The Exordium," "Night," "Daylight,"** and **"Comfort"**

Vocabulary Warm-up Exercises

Exercise A *Fill in the blanks, using each word from Word List A only once.*

After we lost our keynote speaker, we were [1] ________________ to learn that the governor's wife would speak at our fundraiser to help homeless people. She has also offered to give us [2] ________________ about how best to use the money that is raised. The state's first lady is a person of great [3] ________________. She is also [4] ________________ and uses her influence to help others. Her works of [5] ________________ are well known to our community because she has never shied away from helping people in need. She believes that no one should suffer from a difficult [6] ________________. We hope that our combined [7] ________________ to aid the homeless will be successful. We want to attract new donors and encourage former donors to [8] ________________ their contributions.

Exercise B *Answer the questions with complete explanations.*

1. Explain what you would do if your pet went astray.

____

2. Why would you pack varied types of clothing for a trip?

____

3. Would you feel gratified if someone rewarded you for a job well done? Explain.

____

4. Why is it important to be merciful to a person in need?

____

5. If you incurred a great loss of your possessions because of fire, what might you do?

____

6. If someone created a movie about baseball, what resources would he or she need?

____

7. If you abhor candy, would you buy yourself a chocolate bar? Explain.

____

8. Explain why you might need to use good judgment if you are scheduled to travel during stormy weather.

____

Name ______________________________ Date ______________

from the **Qur'an: "The Exordium," "Night," "Daylight,"** and **"Comfort"**

Reading Warm-up A

Read the following passage. Pay special attention to the underlined words. Then, read it again, and complete the activities. Use a separate sheet of paper for your written answers.

Throughout the world, the hajj is a religious journey of great renown. All Muslims and many non-Muslims know about it, and many Muslims make the journey to the city of Mecca each year to celebrate their faith. In fact, each Muslim is required to make the journey at least once in a lifetime. However, people may be relieved from making the hajj for two reasons: if they haven't enough money, or if they are suffering from a serious illness or affliction.

Muslim teaching offers guidance to the faithful about how to perform the hajj. After making certain preparations at home, the pilgrims travel to Mecca, which is in Saudi Arabia. In Mecca, they must perform several endeavors, or projects, related to the hajj.

The parts of the hajj stand for important ideas in the Muslim faith. The pilgrims enter the Holy Mosque at Mecca with the right foot first, and then they recite a prayer as they walk seven times around the mosque in a counter-clockwise direction. Next, the pilgrims go to the city of Mina. There, they run between two small hills seven times. This act represents the story in the Qur'an of Hagar's frantic search for water. The pilgrims then throw seven pebbles at a pillar, an act that represents the story of Abraham's resistance to Satan. Later, a sheep is sacrificed and its meat cooked. The pilgrims must also perform an act of charity with some of the meat, such as giving it to the poor. This requirement represents the importance in Islam of being compassionate and merciful.

The pilgrims then return to Mecca, repeating the prayers and activities performed there earlier. They must also cut their hair as a symbol of completing the hajj before they return home to resume their usual lives.

1. Underline the phrases that explain why the hajj is a journey of great renown. Name a person of great ***renown***.
2. Underline the phrases that explain why people might be relieved from making the hajj. Tell what ***relieved*** means.
3. Circle the word that explains what affliction means. Use ***affliction*** in a sentence.
4. Underline the phrase that explains where a person would find guidance about how to perform the hajj. Tell what ***guidance*** means.
5. Underline the word that helps explain what endeavors means. Use ***endeavors*** in a sentence.
6. Underline the phrase that explains what charity means. Use ***charity*** in a sentence.
7. Underline the word that explains what compassionate means. Tell what ***compassionate*** means.
8. Underline the phrases that explain what resume means. Use ***resume*** in a sentence.

Name ______________________________ Date ______________

***from the* Qur'an: "The Exordium," "Night," "Daylight,"** and **"Comfort"**

Reading Warm-up B

Read the following passage. Pay special attention to the underlined words. Then, read it again, and complete the activities. Use a separate sheet of paper for your written answers.

In the religion of Islam, the Qur'an is the final word of God as expressed by the angel Gabriel to the prophet Muhammad. The structure of the text is varied, containing different types of writing. The Qur'an is the spiritual anchor of millions of Muslims, who believe its teachings surpass all earlier revelations.

Muhammad did not write down the revelations. He chanted them to his followers and later asked them to write the words. However, after Muhammad's death, there was a real danger of losing the Qur'an because many who had committed it to memory died in the battle of al-Yamamah. Scribes were soon employed to record the few written fragments as well as the memories of followers, and these writers created their own order for the text.

The surahs, or chapters, of the Qur'an form the basis of the book and are arranged from longest to shortest. They are divided into two broad categories: those revealed at Mecca and those revealed in Medina. The surahs revealed at Mecca tend to be short and stress the themes of the unity of God, the need for faith, the punishment of those who are led astray from the path of righteousness, and the final judgment by God at which the faithful are rewarded.

The surahs revealed at Medina are longer, and they often deal with specific legal, social, and political situations. All of the surahs are divided into ayahs, or verses, and the Qur'an is subdivided further to facilitate study. With the exception of the ninth, each surah begins with the phrase, "In the Name of God, the Compassionate, the Merciful."

Some Muslim scholars abhor the fact that the Qur'an has been translated into other languages because they think that these translations poorly express the teachings. These scholars argue that outsiders who wish to study the Qur'an have incurred the obligation to read it in the original Arabic. This is time-consuming work for a non-Arabic speaker. Even so, many readers are gratified by the beauty and inspiration that the Qur'an reveals to them.

1. Underline the phrase that helps explain what varied means. Use *varied* in a sentence.
2. Underline the phrase that tells what the scribes created. Explain what *created* means.
3. Circle the phrase that tells how people may be led astray. Use *astray* in a sentence.
4. Underline the word that suggests what judgment means. Use *judgment* in a sentence.
5. Circle the word that means nearly the same as merciful. Use *merciful* in a sentence.
6. Underline the sentence that tells why some scholars abhor translations. Use *abhor* in a sentence.
7. Underline the phrase that tells what has been incurred. Explain what *incurred* means.
8. Why are the scholars gratified to study the surahs? Tell what *gratified* means.

Name ______________________________ Date ______________

from the **Qur'an**

Literary Analysis: Imagery

Imagery is concrete language intended to appeal to the senses; **images** are individual examples of imagery. Vivid images help the reader imagine how the thing being described looks, sounds, smells, tastes, or feels. In the Qur'an, imagery paints vivid pictures of such abstract concepts as "mercy" and "righteousness" in order to enable the believer to imagine them.

DIRECTIONS: *Complete the following chart. Explain what sense each image appeals to. Then, indicate the concept that the image helps to paint a word picture of and the effect of portraying the concept with this particular image.*

Image	Sense(s) Appealed To	Concept Portrayed	Effect of the Imagery
1. "the straight path" (The Exordium)			
2. "when she lets fall her darkness" ("Night")			
3. "We shall smooth the path of affliction" ("Night")			
4. "I warn you, then, of the blazing Fire" ("Night")			
5. "Did He not find you an orphan and give you shelter?" ("Daylight")			

Name ______________________________ Date ______________

from the **Qur'an**

Reading Strategy: Set a Purpose for Reading

Setting a purpose for reading means deciding before you read something why you are reading it and what you want to concentrate on as you read. For example, if you are reading about a scientific experiment, your purpose might be to determine what theory the scientist was testing, or your purpose might be to find out what steps the experimenter followed. Setting a purpose for reading makes it easier to process and remember the information you are taking in, because, in a sense, you have already prepared a structure for it in your mind.

DIRECTIONS: *Before you read the following paragraph about the Five Pillars of Wisdom, write a purpose for yourself. Your purpose might be to learn more about one of the Pillars or to learn how the Pillars came to be the basis for Muslim conduct. As you read the paragraph, underline the most relevant sentences. Then, answer the questions that follow.*

My purpose for reading: ______________________________

The Five Pillars of Wisdom

The Five Pillars of the Muslim religion form a code of behavior that all Muslims are expected to follow. The Five Pillars include expressing the basic Muslim creed, praying five times a day, giving alms to the poor, fasting during Ramadan, and making a pilgrimage to Mecca. The first Pillar involves believing in and proclaiming the Muslim creed: "There is no God but Allah; Muhammad is His prophet." Prayer, the second Pillar, is undertaken five times a day: at daybreak, at noon, in the afternoon, in the evening, and at nightfall. Before praying, Muslims wash their face, hands, and feet. Almsgiving involves both mandatory donation, known as Zakat, which requires Muslims to give 2.5 percent of their income to charity, and voluntary giving, called Sadaqah. During the holy month of Ramadan, Muslims are required to refrain from eating and drinking every day from sunrise to sunset, with exceptions for travelers, people who are ill, soldiers on duty, and nursing mothers. The end of Ramadan is celebrated in the three-day Festival of the Breaking of the Fast. Each Muslim is required to make at least one pilgrimage to the holy city of Mecca during his or her lifetime. The pilgrimage includes a number of ceremonies, such as walking seven times around the Kaaba, Mecca's sacred shrine, and kissing the sacred Black Stone in its wall.

1. Which sentences were most relevant to your purpose?

   ____

2. What is the most important piece of information that you learned from the paragraph?

   ____

3. Now that you know the content of the paragraph, narrow your purpose for reading to something more specific.

   ____

Name ______________________ Date ______________

from the Qur'an

Vocabulary Builder

Using the Latin Prefix *ab-*

The Latin prefix *ab-* means "away" or "from." For example, *abhor* literally means to "shrink from in disgust."

A. DIRECTIONS: *In each of the following sentences, use the correct word from the box.*

abdicate	absolve	abolish

1. The king chose to ______________ his throne rather than give up the woman he loved.
2. Congress voted to ______________ several government bureaus.
3. Saying you're sorry does not necessarily ______________ you of the offense.

Using the Word List

compassionate	affliction	abhor	renown
incurred	recompense	chide	fervor

B. DIRECTIONS: *Match the Word List words on the left with their meanings on the right. Write the letter of each answer on the line.*

___ 1. incurred — A. payment of what is owed
___ 2. abhor — B. fame
___ 3. recompense — C. brought about oneself
___ 4. chide — D. to hate
___ 5. renown — E. to scold

C. DIRECTIONS: *Write the letter of the word that best completes each analogy.*

1. NIGHT : DAY :: affliction :
   A. health B. fondness C. cold D. forgiveness
2. HATRED : ABHORRENCE :: fervor :
   A. maliciousness B. preference C. zeal D. sorrow
3. APPROVE : CONSENT :: chide :
   A. scold B. punish C. recompense D. misbehave

Name ______________________ Date ______________

from the **Qur'an**

Grammar and Style: Parallelism

Parallelism refers to the presentation of similar ideas in similar grammatical structures. Writers use parallelism in order to express related ideas.

Parallel: Religious activities include prayer, meditation, and participation in rituals.

Not parallel: Religious activities include prayer, to meditate, and participating in rituals.

Parallelism makes writing easier to follow because it establishes a pattern that helps structure the words and support their meanings. Parallelism also makes writing more memorable, powerful, rhythmic, and fluid.

A. PRACTICE: *Several of the following sentences include expressions that are not parallel. On the line provided, rewrite the sentences that need to be revised. For those sentences that are parallel, write* Correct *on the line.*

1. Muhammad continued receiving revelations from the age of forty until he died.

____

____

2. Surahs vary in length from three or four verses to some that are more than 200 verses.

____

____

3. Muhammad is viewed not as the author but as the one who transmitted Allah's message.

____

____

4. Muslims are expected to perform the following five acts of worship: reciting the creed, praying five times a day, giving charity to the poor, fasting during Ramadan, and making at least one pilgrimage to Mecca.

____

____

B. Writing Application: *Write four sentences about the things you value most, using parallelism in each sentence.*

1. ______________________
2. ______________________
3. ______________________
4. ______________________

Name ______________________ Date ______________

from the **Qur'an**

Support for Writing

To help you create your own guidelines for **personal behavior**, use the following chart to organize your thoughts in the prewriting stage. Fill in the first column of the chart with five or six human qualities that seem important to you. Then, fill in the second column with the kind of behavior that you think reflects each quality.

Important Human Qualities	Related Kinds of Behavior
1.	
2.	
3.	
4.	
5.	
6.	

Now, use your notes to write your guidelines for personal behavior.

Name ______________________ Date ______________

from the **Qur'an**

Support for Extend Your Learning

Listening and Speaking

To prepare for your **speech** on what *compassion* and *mercy* mean to you, use the following graphic organizer to help you define each word and provide examples of it. Then, use this information in an opening statement that addresses the importance of these two concepts.

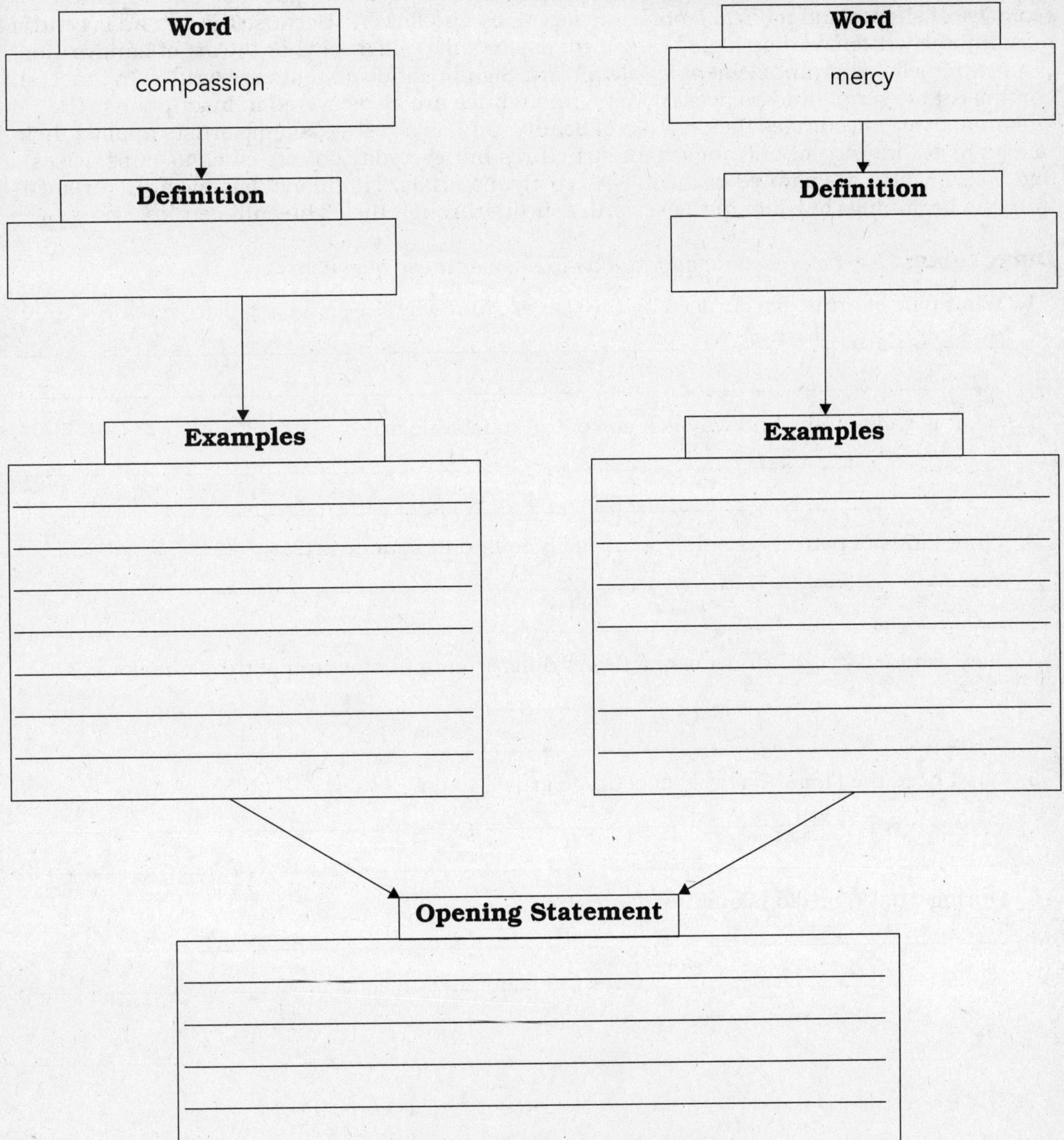

Name ______________________________ Date ______________

from the **Qur'an**

Enrichment: Islamic Art

Islamic art is highly patterned and extremely beautiful. The Qur'an itself discourages naturalistic representation, because such art might be confused with idol making, which is strictly forbidden in Islam. However, Islamic art is full of brilliant stylized (that is, more patterned than naturalistic) images from nature, as well as abstract patterns intricate in design and rich in color. Surfaces of buildings and objects are covered with patterns that repeat geometrical shapes and natural motifs, such as vines and flowers. Because the Qur'an is central to Islam, the written word is highly esteemed; as a result, calligraphy, or the art of handwriting, is an extremely important element in Islamic art. Significant documents are written in graceful, curving Arabic script, and palaces, pottery, and fabrics are also covered in inscriptions. The Qur'an actively encourages the creation of beauty, and as a result, Islamic artists applied their talents to decorating not only important structures but everyday objects, such as cups, vases, and boxes, which are painted or inlaid with costly materials. Traditional Islamic art flourished from the beginnings of Islam in the seventh century through the eighteenth century.

DIRECTIONS: *Use the preceding information to answer these questions.*

1. What type of art is discouraged by the Qur'an, and why?

____

____

2. What is calligraphy, and why is it so central to Islamic art?

____

____

3. What kinds of patterns would you be likely to find in Islamic art?

____

____

4. How would a stylized drawing of a flower differ from a photograph of the same flower?

____

____

5. What does the Qur'an actively encourage artists to do?

____

____

6. During what time did Islamic art flourish?

____

____

Name ______________________________ Date ______________

from the **Qur'an**

Selection Test A

Critical Reading *Identify the letter of the choice that best answers the question.*

____ 1. Which would be a purpose for reading the Qur'an?
A. to hear about Muhammad
B. to learn how to live in the desert
C. to read about family life in ancient times
D. to understand Islamic values

____ 2. Who is the "You" in "The Exordium" section of the Qur'an?
A. the reader
B. Muhammad
C. God
D. Earth

____ 3. Which sense is used to speak about "darkness, and . . . the radiant day" in "Night" from the Qur'an?
A. sight
B. touch
C. smell
D. taste

____ 4. What kind of man does good works to please the "Most High" in "Night" from the Qur'an?
A. a selfish man
B. a good man
C. a humorous man
D. a powerful man

____ 5. To which sense does the idea of smoothing a path to salvation appeal in "Night" from the Qur'an?
A. touch
B. taste
C. smell
D. hearing

____ 6. Which of God's qualities does the Qur'an suggest in this passage from "Daylight"?
Did He not find you an orphan and give you shelter?
A. mystery
B. forgiveness
C. kindness
D. strength

Name ____________________ Date ____________

____ 7. What does the Qur'an suggest in "Daylight" by contrasting "the life to come" with "this present life"?
A. There is more than one God.
B. There is an afterlife.
C. There is kindness in the world.
D. There is evil in the world.

____ 8. Why might someone choose to read the "Comfort" section of the Qur'an?
A. to understand how the universe began
B. to feel better during a difficult time
C. to get advice about a job search
D. to learn about a religion

____ 9. What does the "Comfort" section of the Qur'an suggest about Allah's prophet?
A. God will lift up God's heart.
B. The reader will have hardship.
C. Muhammad will be helped.
D. The burden will grow heavy.

____ 10. Which image from the Qur'an appeals most strongly to the sense of touch?
A. the radiant day
B. the beggar
C. the goodness
D. the blazing Fire

____ 11. What is the effect of repeating "With every hardship there is ease" in "Comfort" from the Qur'an?
A. The reader feels surprised.
B. The reader feels upset.
C. The reader feels better.
D. The reader feels doubt.

Vocabulary and Grammar

____ 12. If you have an *affliction,* which professional person would you want to see?
A. mechanic
B. doctor
C. lawyer
D. teacher

____ 13. Which word is most nearly **opposite** in meaning to the word *abhor*?
A. love
B. hate
C. yell
D. whisper

Name ______________________ Date ______________________

14. Which example from the Qur'an shows parallelism, or similar structure in two places?
   A. But proclaim the goodness of your Lord.
   B. Have We not given you High renown?
   C. You alone we worship, and to You alone we turn for help.
   D. When your prayers are ended resume your toil, and seek your Lord.

15. Which word or phrase should be added to make this sentence grammatically parallel?
   The Qur'an portrays the Lord as powerful, fair, and ______.
   A. full of kindness
   B. kind
   C. a Lord who has kindness
   D. showing kindness

Essay

16. According to the sections of the Qur'an that you read, what are the main qualities of God? Develop your ideas in an essay supported by examples from "The Exordium," "Night," "Daybreak," and "Comfort."

17. How does the Qur'an make use of sensory images to convey its message? Develop your ideas in an essay supported by examples from the Qur'an.

Name ________________________________ Date ________________

from the Qur'an

Selection Test B

Critical Reading *Identify the letter of the choice that best completes the the question.*

____ 1. Whom does the Exordium to the Qur'an directly address?
A. God
B. the faithful
C. the Prophet
D. no one

____ 2. What image does the Exordium use to convey the idea of right behavior?
A. a bright light
B. a beautiful room
C. a straight path
D. a valuable prize

____ 3. According to "Night," all but which of the following will help one achieve salvation?
A. giving in charity
B. guarding against evil
C. seeking recompense for good works
D. believing in goodness

____ 4. According to "Night," what will happen only to the "hardened sinner"?
A. He will repent and be saved.
B. He will burn in a blazing fire.
C. He will lose his way and perish.
D. He will die in poverty.

____ 5. If your purpose in reading "Night" is to learn about Islamic ethics, which action should you understand to be virtuous?
A. disbelief in goodness
B. working for a good cause
C. self-sacrifice
D. studying

____ 6. To which senses does the image of "the blazing fire" appeal?
A. sight and touch
B. sight and hearing
C. touch and taste
D. sight, taste, and hearing

____ 7. What idea of God do the following images from "Daylight" emphasize?

Did He not find you an orphan and give you shelter? / Did He not find you in error and guide you? / Did He not find you poor and enrich you?

A. He is a just and demanding taskmaster.
B. He is the creator of all things.
C. He is an all-powerful deity.
D. He is a benevolent and loving deity.

Name ______________________ Date ______________

____ 8. According to "Daylight," what has the Lord NOT done?
A. He has not forsaken you.
B. He has not given you shelter.
C. He has not enriched you.
D. He has not guided you.

____ 9. What is the effect of the repetition of this line in "Comfort": "With every hardship there is ease"?
A. consolation
B. discouragement
C. instruction
D. doubt

____ 10. According to the background material, what was the home of the Mohammed?
A. the desert
B. Persia
C. Mecca
D. Cairo

____ 11. Which of the following would NOT be a purpose for reading the surahs of the Qur'an?
A. to learn more about the life of Mohammed
B. to identify Islamic virtues
C. to explore the relationship between God and humanity
D. to appreciate the language of the scripture

Vocabulary and Grammar

____ 12. In the following lines from the Exordium to the Qur'an, what does the word *incurred* mean?

Guide us to the straight path, / The path of those whom You have favoured, / Not of those who have incurred Your wrath, / Nor of those who have gone astray.

A. avoided
B. caused
C. healed
D. frightened

____ 13. If you have an *affliction,* whom would you want to see?
A. a physician
B. a banker
C. a chef
D. a cleaning service

____ 14. Which word contains a Latin prefix meaning "away"?
A. compassionate
B. incurred
C. renown
D. abhor

Name ________________________ Date ________________

____ 15. What is the meaning of the word *recompense* in the following sentence?

But the good man . . . shall keep away from [punishment]:, and so shall he that does good works for the sake of the Most High only, seeking no recompense.

A. payment
B. evil
C. faith
D. followers

____ 16. Which of the following statements uses parallel structure?

A. "We shall smooth the path of salvation."
B. "When he breathes his last, his riches will not avail him."
C. "But the good man who keeps himself pure by almsgiving shall keep away from it."
D. "your Lord has not forsaken you, nor does he abhor you."

____ 17. In order for the following sentence to be parallel, which word or phrase should be added?

According to the Qur'an, God is just, righteous, protective, and ______ .

A. full of compassion
B. shows compassion
C. compassionate
D. a compassionate Lord

Essay

18. What qualities of God are emphasized in the Exordium and the surahs that you have read? Support your ideas with evidence from the Exordium, "Night," "Daybreak," and "Comfort."

19. The Qur'an uses a number of images to make abstract concepts more concrete and easier to understand. Write a brief essay about one of the following images from the portions of the Qur'an that you read: "Sovereign of the Day of Judgement," "the straight path," "the blazing Fire," the prize of the life to come, an orphan, the burden. What is the image used to describe it in the Qur'an, and what is its meaning? What impressions does it create for you?

20. If you were to read more of the Qur'an, what would your purpose be? Base your answer on the excerpts you have read in this grouping. For example, you might want to see whether the ideas you came across here are repeated often in the other surahs, or you might wish to find out whether other qualities of God's are portrayed elsewhere in the Qur'an. Compose your response in a brief essay.

from **The Thousand and One Nights: "The Fisherman and the Jinnee"**

Vocabulary Warm-up Word Lists

Study these words from the selection. Then, complete the activities.

Word List A

bestow [bi STOH] *v.* give as a gift or honor
The guests came to bestow gifts upon the child for his birthday.

consequences [KON si kwens es] *n.* results
One of the consequences of our prank was that we were punished for it.

doubtless [DOWT luhs] *adv.* definitely; certainly
She was doubtless the most talented musician in the band.

jinn [jin] *n.* in Middle Eastern stories, spirits with supernatural powers
The three jinn told us that they would each grant us three wishes.

lamentations [lam uhn TAY shuhns] *n.* expressions of sadness or grief
Bob's lamentations about missing his favorite television show were heard by all of us.

resolutely [REZ uh loot lee] *adv.* firmly; done in a determined way
Sharon resolutely denied taking the last cookie, and we believed her.

resumed [ri ZOOMD] *v.* started again after an interruption
We resumed our conversation after the film ended.

venom [VEN uhm] *n.* poison
The venom of a rattlesnake is deadly.

Word List B

arteries [AR tuh reez] *n.* blood vessels in the body that carry blood away from the heart
There are many arteries in the body through which the blood circulates.

aspect [AS pekt] *n.* part; what something looks like when seen from a certain angle
The best aspect of Jane's personality is her sense of humor.

bounteous [BOWN tee us] *adj.* plentiful; abundant; giving in great quantity
The bounteous harvest means that no one in the village will go hungry this winter.

embrace [em BRAYS] *v.* hug; hold with the arms
Sally will embrace John when he returns from his trip around the world.

endeavors [en DEV uhrs] *n.* projects; hard work toward a goal
Peter's artistic endeavors led him to a job as a cartoonist.

motive [MOH tiv] *n.* a reason for an action
His motive for the crime was his need for money.

prophet [PRAHF it] *n.* a person who predicts the future
The prophet predicted that we would have good fortune.

proverb [PRAHV uhrb] *n.* a short saying that expresses a truth
My father recites a proverb to me when he wants to give me advice.

Name ______________________ Date ______________

from **The Thousand and One Nights: "The Fisherman and the Jinnee"**

Vocabulary Warm-up Exercises

Exercise A *Fill in each blank in the paragraph below with an appropriate word from Word List A. Use each word only once.*

A man interrupted us and told us that two [1] ______________ would appear before us from his bottle. They would [2] ______________ two wishes upon us. The man promised us that we would not suffer any negative [3] ______________ from making these wishes. We [4] ______________ refused to make any wishes. We remembered the [5] ______________ of our friend whose wishes resulted in disaster. With [6] ______________ in our voices, we told the man to take his bottle and leave. [7] ______________, the man had expected us to accept his offer. After he left, we [8] ______________ the work we were doing before we were interrupted.

Exercise B *Answer the questions with complete explanations.*

1. List one motive that you have for saving your money.
____
2. Name one proverb that inspires you.
____
3. If you could be a prophet, what is one positive event that you would like to predict?
____
4. Should you embrace someone who has a cold? Why or why not?
____
5. What is the nicest aspect of your personality?
____
6. If you planned to go camping this weekend only, would you need a bounteous amount of supplies? Why or why not?
____
7. Name one endeavor that you must take on in order get good grades.
____
8. Why are arteries an important part of the body?
____

Name ______________________________ Date ______________

from **The Thousand and One Nights: "The Fisherman and the Jinnee"**

Reading Warm-up A

Read the following passage. Pay special attention to the underlined words. Then, read it again, and complete the activities. Use a separate sheet of paper for your written answers.

As Charles entered the house, he firmly made up his mind. He was resolutely determined not to look upset. Even though he tried hard to be cheerful, his family could tell that he was upset about something. After dinner, Charles sadly voiced his lamentations to us.

"I really wish some jinn would appear before me right now and grant me a few wishes," he said. "I had a terrible day yesterday. I got stuck in traffic, and as a result, I did not get a job."

"What happened?" his sister, Amy, asked.

"You've doubtless heard about the monstrous traffic jam that occurred on the highway yesterday. It was covered by the evening news, and it was reported in all of today's papers," Charles began. "Well, I was stuck in it and one of the consequences was that I arrived too late for my job interview."

Charles' mother felt sorry for him because she knew that he really wanted that job. Now, he would have to apply for another one.

"Have you resumed your job search?" she asked.

"No, and I don't want to start again. It's useless!" Charles replied. "You should have seen how the manager looked at me when I arrived late. He looked so angry when he spoke to me that I knew he disliked me. If he were a cobra, he would have spit venom at me. He told me to get out because the position was already filled. I tried to explain that I was late because of the accident, but he wouldn't listen."

"If I could bestow good luck upon you, I would," his mother said. "However, I can't give you luck. The best that I can do is offer you my assistance."

"Me, too," Sarah said.

Charles looked at his mother and sister. He realized that he was indeed lucky to have such a supportive family.

"Okay," he said, smiling. "How about we start the job search again tomorrow morning?"

1. Underline the phrase that is a clue to the meaning of resolutely. What qualities can help a person act *resolutely*?
2. Underline the word that is a clue to the meaning of *lamentations*. Tell what ***lamentations*** means.
3. Underline the phrase that tells what jinn do. Use ***jinn*** in a sentence.
4. Underline the sentence that explains why Sarah doubtless heard about the huge traffic jam. Tell what ***doubtless*** means.
5. Underline the phrase that tells one of the consequences that Charles suffered. Tell what ***consequences*** means.
6. Circle the phrase that means nearly the same as resumed. Use resumed in a sentence.
7. Underline the word that names a creature that has venom. Use ***venom*** in a sentence.
8. Underline the word that means nearly the same as bestow. Tell what ***bestow*** means.

Name ______________________________ Date ______________

from The Thousand and One Nights: "The Fisherman and the Jinnee"

Reading Warm-up B

Read the following passage. Pay special attention to the underlined words. Then, read it again, and complete the activities. Use a separate sheet of paper for your written answers.

The image of the jinnee has been extremely popular in literature and culture. This image is found in ancient Arabic and Muslim literature. However, there are also bounteous examples of the jinnee's popularity today. Among these many examples, a good number can be found in American popular culture.

In traditional Muslim belief, the jinnee is a spirit that lives on the earth and can take on a human or animal aspect. The jinnee can be good or evil. Arabic literature has many examples of the jinnee.

One well-known example of a jinnee is found in the tale of Aladdin and the Lamp. In one version of that story, a magician pretends to be Aladdin's uncle. He says he has come to help Aladdin, who is very poor, but he magician's real motive is to make Aladdin get a magic lamp for him. This lamp will make the magician very powerful. However, the magician fails in his endeavors. Despite his efforts, Aladdin keeps the lamp. Aladdin eventually lives happily ever after because the genie grants his wishes.

No prophet could have predicted how popular the jinnee would become in American culture. In fact, it can be said that the idea of the jinnee brings to life the old proverb, "Ask and you shall receive." Americans have come to embrace the jinnee because it is the symbol of having dreams come true. Just as the blood travels through the arteries of the body, this idea has traveled through many cultural roads. It is seen in popular music, television shows, and film versions of the story of Aladdin and his Magic Lamp. Whatever the reason for its popularity, the jinnee has captured the imaginations of many people over the centuries.

1. Circle the word that means nearly the same as bounteous. Use ***bounteous*** in a sentence.
2. Circle the words that describe the aspect that a jinnee can take on. Describe something that has more than one ***aspect***.
3. Underline the phrase that explains the motive behind the magician's efforts to help Aladdin. Tell what ***motive*** means.
4. Underline the phrase that is a clue to the meaning of endeavors. Use ***endeavors*** in a sentence.
5. Circle the word that tells what a prophet does. Use ***prophet*** in a sentence.
6. Underline the proverb that describes the idea of the jinnee in American culture. Tell what ***proverb*** means.
7. Underline the phrase that tells why Americans have come to embrace the jinnee. Tell what ***embrace*** means.
8. Underline the phrase that helps to explain what arteries means. Use ***arteries*** in a sentence.

Name ______________________________ Date ______________

***from* The Thousand and One Nights: "The Fisherman and the Jinnee"**

Literary Analysis: Folk Tales

Folk tales are stories that have been passed down for generations by word of mouth. Folk tales often contain lessons about life, one-dimensional characters (characters who display only one or two traits), supernatural or magical elements, clear separation of good and evil, and weak characters who use trickery to outsmart the strong.

DIRECTIONS: *Find examples of each element of a folk tale in one of the three interlocking tales that make up "The Fisherman and the Jinnee." Write your examples in the right-hand column.*

Element	Example
1. lesson about life	
2. one-dimensional characters	
3. supernatural or magical elements	
4. clear separation of good and evil	
5. trickery	

Name ______________________ Date ______________

***from* The Thousand and One Nights: "The Fisherman and the Jinnee"**

Reading Strategy: Summarize

When you **summarize,** or create a summary, you state the main ideas or events and key supporting details in your own words. Summarizing can help you understand a work, remember it better, and communicate information about it to others.

DIRECTIONS: *On the following modified outline, list main events and key supporting details that you would include in a summary of the main story about the fisherman and the jinnee. You do not have to fill in every line, but make sure that you include all the important information in the story.*

Main Idea or Event: ______________________

Supporting Detail: ______________________

Supporting Detail: ______________________

Supporting Detail: ______________________

Supporting Detail: ______________________

Main Idea or Event: ______________________

Supporting Detail: ______________________

Supporting Detail: ______________________

Supporting Detail: ______________________

Supporting Detail: ______________________

Main Idea or Event: ______________________

Supporting Detail: ______________________

Supporting Detail: ______________________

Supporting Detail: ______________________

Supporting Detail: ______________________

Name ______________________________ Date ______________

from **The Thousand and One Nights: "The Fisherman and the Jinnee"**

Vocabulary Builder

Using the Latin Root *-vert-*

The Latin root *-vert-* means "turn." It occurs in the word *inverted,* which means "turned upside down or inside out."

A. DIRECTIONS: *Explain how the meaning of the root -vert- figures into the meaning of each of the following words. Consult a dictionary if necessary.*

1. introvert: ______________________________
2. extrovert: ______________________________
3. vertigo: ______________________________
4. convert: ______________________________
5. revert: ______________________________

Using the Word List

inverted	adjured	resolutely	munificence
blasphemous	indignantly	enraptured	ominous

B. DIRECTIONS: *Using your knowledge of the Word List words, decide whether each statement below is true or false. On the line before the statement, write* T *if the statement is true. Write* F *if it is false.*

___ 1. An *inverted* glass has its rim face down on the surface.

___ 2. If someone *adjured* you to do something, he or she probably made you laugh.

___ 3. Most people admire *blasphemous* behavior.

___ 4. Someone listening to the most beautiful music might be *enraptured.*

___ 5. A person behaving with *munificence* might make a donation to charity.

C. DIRECTIONS: *Write the letter of the synonym of each Word List word.*

___ 1. enraptured A. clawed B. entranced C. deprived D. torn

___ 2. ominous A. bright B. tiny C. threatening D. charming

___ 3. munificence A. beauty B. generosity C. elegance D. peace

___ 4. resolutely A. stubbornly B. flexibly C. completely D. helpfully

___ 5. indignantly A. scornfully B. subtly C. deeply D. oddly

Name ______________________________ Date ______________

from **The Thousand and One Nights: "The Fisherman and the Jinnee"**

Grammar and Style: Action Verbs and Linking Verbs

Action verbs express physical or mental action. **Linking verbs** express a state of being and are usually followed by a noun or pronoun that renames the subject or by an adjective that describes it. Only a handful of verbs can be used as linking verbs. They include *appear, be (is, are, was,* and so on*), become, feel, grow, look, remain, seem, smell, sound, stay, taste,* and *turn.* Several of these verbs can also be action verbs, depending on how they are used.

Action Verb: The fisherman *looked* at the jinnee. **Linking Verb:** The jinnee *looked* scary.

To figure out whether a verb is a linking verb, see whether (a) it is followed by a noun or pronoun that renames the subject or by an adjective that describes it or whether (b) a form of *be* (*is, was,* and so on) can replace the verb without drastically changing the meaning of the sentence. For instance, in the second sample sentence above, the verb *looked* is followed by an adjective, *scary,* that describes the subject, *jinnee;* if you replace *looked* with *was,* the meaning of the sentence hardly changes. Therefore, *looked* is a linking verb. The same tests show that in the first sample sentence, *looked* is not a linking verb but an action verb.

A. Practice: *Circle the verb in each sentence. Then, on the line, write* A *if the verb is an action verb or* L *if the verb is a linking verb.*

____ 1. One day a poor fisherman tossed his net out very far into the sea.

____ 2. Soon the net felt very heavy.

____ 3. The fisherman hauled a mysterious bottle back to shore.

____ 4. He felt the bottle with both hands.

B. Writing Application: *Follow the instructions for writing sentences that contain either an action verb or a linking verb.*

1. Use a form of *be* to describe the fisherman.

____

2. Use *look* as an action verb in a sentence about Duban the Doctor.

____

3. Use *look* as a linking verb in a sentence about the jinnee's appearance.

____

4. Use *appear* as an action verb in a sentence about the jinnee's bottle.

____

5. Use *grow* as a linking verb to describe King Sindbad's reaction to the falcon.

____

Name ______________________________ Date ______________

from **The Thousand and One Nights: "The Fisherman and the Jinnee"**

Support for Writing

Use the chart below to organize your notes about details of "The Fisherman and the Jinnee" that could appeal to readers of different cultures and different times.

Details That Appeal to Readers of Different Cultures	Details That Appeal to Readers of Different Times

Opening Statement About the Story's Enduring Appeal

Then, use your notes as a basis for writing a brief critique about the story's enduring appeal.

Name ______________________________ Date ______________

from **The Thousand and One Nights: "The Fisherman and the Jinnee"**

Support for Extend Your Learning

Research and Technology

Use the chart below to record information for your written **report** about jinnees and their role in Persian and Middle Eastern folklore.

Jinnees' Role in Persian Folklore	Jinnes' Role in Middle Eastern Folklore

Listening and Speaking

Use the following set of questions to guide your planning of a **panel discussion** of Rimsky-Korsakov's work *Scheherazade* and how well it evokes the mood of *The Thousand and One Nights*.

1. Where can I obtain a CD version of *Scheherazade*? At a music store? At the library?

 ____

2. If I find several versions, should I listen to them to see which one I like best? What qualities should I look for in the performance?

 ____

 ____

3. Should I divide the musical work and discussion into sections, or should I play the music without interruption and have the panel discuss the work as a whole?

 ____

 ____

4. Should we take questions and comments from the class? Why or why not?

 ____

 ____

Name ______________________________ Date ______________

***from* The Thousand and One Nights: "The Fisherman and the Jinnee"**

Enrichment: Supernatural Creatures

The folk literature of many cultures features supernatural spirits who involve themselves in human affairs. Such creatures, who often take on human or animal form, frequently lurk in natural or manmade objects like trees, rivers, boulders, lamps, and bottles, waiting for some hapless human being to come along. Though they may offer good things, like wealth or the granting of wishes, these benefits invariably come with drawbacks. Sometimes the humans use their wits to profit in spite of the drawbacks; sometimes they fail to reap the benefits. The jinn (plural of *jinnee*) of Persian and Arabian literature are one illustration of this sort of creature; other examples include the trolls of Scandinavian folklore; the leprechauns of Irish folklore, and the kappa of Japanese folklore.

DIRECTIONS: *Answers these questions on the lines provided.*

1. In involving himself in human affairs, what benefits has the jinnee sometimes offered, and what harm does he now bring?

____

____

2. When the fisherman encounters him, where is the jinnee lurking, and how did he get there?

____

____

3. Would you say that jinnee takes on human form? Why or why not?

____

____

4. How does the fisherman get the better of jinnee? Does he reap any material benefits from the encounter? What lesson about life might this outcome suggest?

____

____

____

____

5. Why might mischievous supernatural creatures be popular in folklore the world over?

____

____

____

____

____

____

Name ______________________________ Date ______________

from The Thousand and One Nights: "The Fisherman and the Jinnee"

Selection Test A

Critical Reading *Identify the letter of the choice that best answers the question.*

____ 1. The jinnee in "The Fisherman and the Jinnee" is an example of which characteristic of a folk tale?
- A. a lesson about life
- B. a magical or supernatural element
- C. a character who is like a king
- D. a separation between good and evil

____ 2. What is the relationship of the three folk tales that make up "The Fisherman and the Jinnee"?
- A. King Yunan tells about Sindbad, who tells about the fisherman.
- B. The fisherman tells about King Yunan, who tells about King Sindbad.
- C. King Sindbad tells about the fisherman, who tells about King Yunan.
- D. King Sindbad tells about King Yunan, who tells about the fisherman.

____ 3. Why did the jinnee swear to kill the man who freed him in "The Fisherman and the Jinnee"?
- A. The jinnee was angry at him.
- B. The jinnee missed his family.
- C. The jinnee was relieved to be free.
- D. The jinee was tired of waiting to be freed.

____ 4. In "The Fisherman and the Jinnee," how many of the tales pay back "good [deeds] with evil"?
- A. none
- B. one
- C. two
- D. all of them

____ 5. In which tale of "The Fisherman and the Jinnee" does cleverness help the weak person escape harm?
- A. The fisherman and the jinnee
- B. King Yunan and Duban
- C. King Sindbad and the falcon
- D. none of the tales

____ 6. Why does the falcon keep knocking over the bowl of liquid in "The Fisherman and the Jinnee"?
- A. The falcon likes to tease the king.
- B. The falcon is jealous of the king.
- C. The falcon wants to misbehave.
- D. The falcon wants to save the king.

Name ______________________________ Date ____________________

___ 7. Which phrase best summarizes the falcon's attitude in "The Fisherman and the Jinnee"?
A. jealous of King Sindbad
B. greedy for King Sindbad's wealth
C. loyal to King Sindbad
D. cruel to King Sindbad

___ 8. How does King Sindbad behave when he attacks the falcon in "The Fisherman and the Jinnee"?
A. He is fair and reasonable.
B. He is easily frightened.
C. He cannot control his anger.
D. He acts calmly.

___ 9. In "The Fisherman and the Jinnee," why does King Yunan talk about King Sindbad and the falcon?
A. to teach the vizier a lesson
B. to surprise the vizier
C. to help the vizier sleep
D. to impress the vizier

___ 10. How does King Yunan behave toward the doctor in "The Fisherman and the Jinnee"?
A. His gratitude is stronger than his fears.
B. His fears are stronger than his gratitude.
C. His kindness is stronger than his selfishness.
D. His trickery is stronger than his gratitude.

___ 11. What effect do the doctor's final instructions have on King Yunan in "The Fisherman and the Jinnee"?
A. The king obeys them and is poisoned.
B. The king obeys them and is cured.
C. The king obeys them and is put in prison.
D. The king obeys them and is freed.

Vocabulary and Grammar

___ 12. Which word is most nearly **opposite** in meaning to *blasphemous*?
A. frightening
B. comforting
C. holy
D. evil

___ 13. Which statement from "The Fisherman and the Jinnee" is an example of *munificence*?
A. King Sindbad attacks the falcon.
B. King Sindbad grieves for his falcon.
C. King Yunan has the doctor beheaded.
D. King Yunan gives the doctor gold.

Name ______________________ Date ______________

___ 14. Which sentence from "The Fisherman and the Jinnee" contains a linking verb?
A. The jinnee trembled at the mention of the Name.
B. Then the King gave him a robe of honor.
C. He is my friend.
D. I speak of Duban, the doctor.

___ 15. Which is the action verb in this sentence: "The King had not turned six pages . . ."?
A. six
B. King
C. pages
D. turned

Essay

16. In an essay, summarize the plot and key details of "The Tale of King Yunan and Duban the Doctor" from "The Fisherman and the Jinnee." Use only necessary details to make your summary concise.

17. Choose one of the three folk tales in "The Fisherman and the Jinnee." In a brief essay, explain the lesson it teaches about life. Use examples from the selection to support your explanation.

Name ______________________________ Date ______________

from **The Thousand and One Nights: "The Fisherman and the Jinnee"**

Selection Test B

Critical Reading *Identify the letter of the choice that best completes the question.*

____ 1. Which statement best describes the relationship of the three folk tales that make up "The Fisherman and the Jinnee"?
- A. A character in the first story tells a second story in which a character tells a third story.
- B. The first story explains the characters' plight in the second story, which in turn explains the characters' plight in the third story.
- C. All three stories feature characters who are members of the same extended family.
- D. All three stories trace the adventures of different members of King Yunan's court.

____ 2. Which character trait leads the fisherman to discover the jinnee?
- A. curiosity
- B. wisdom
- C. resentment
- D. compassion

____ 3. When the fisherman releases the jinnee, what is the jinnee planning to give to anyone who helps him escape the bottle?
- A. riches
- B. death
- C. the secret to immortality
- D. the means to travel to exotic places

____ 4. Which sentence gives the best summary of the jinnee's background?
- A. He was the leader of the giants who fought in the armies of King Solomon, prophet of Allah.
- B. He was imprisoned in a bottle after disobeying a king.
- C. He was a rebel jinnee whom King Solomon imprisoned in a bottle and had cast into the sea because the jinnee refused to accept Solomon's religion.
- D. He was a rebel jinnee who, along with Sakhr the Jinnee, mutinied against King Solomon, who then sent for several faithful jinn, who carried the bottle away and cast it into the middle of the sea.

____ 5. What is one major difference between the jinnee and the fisherman?
- A. The fisherman is foolish; the jinnee is clever.
- B. The fisherman is wealthy; the jinnee is poor.
- C. The fisherman is religious; the jinnee is blasphemous.
- D. The fisherman is an influential member of society; the jinnee is a despised outsider.

____ 6. What motivates King Yunan's vizier to speak ill of Duban the Doctor?
- A. He suspects Duban is plotting against the king.
- B. He fears Duban will poison him in order to take his place as the king's advisor.
- C. He is afraid the clever doctor will uncover his plot to overthrow the king.
- D. He is jealous of the doctor's favor with the king.

____ 7. Why does King Yunan decide to kill Duban?

Name ______________________ Date ______________

A. He discovers that the doctor has given him a poisoned book.
B. He is furious when his leprosy returns.
C. He learns that the doctor and the vizier are plotting together to overthrow him.
D. He becomes convinced that the doctor is trying to kill him.

____ 8. How are the jinnee and King Yunan alike?
A. Both derive their power from magic.
B. Both unfairly seek to punish an innocent person.
C. Both understand how to outsmart an opponent.
D. Both unwisely follow the advice of a vizier.

____ 9. What lesson about life does "The Tale of King Yunan and Duban the Doctor" most clearly convey?
A. It is important to maintain traditions.
B. People with power should be merciful.
C. A good leader is harsh but fair.
D. Remain strong through adversity.

____ 10. If you were summarizing "The Tale of King Sindbad and the Falcon," which of these details would you be *least* likely to include?
A. The king goes hunting with the falcon.
B. A gazelle falls into the king's snare.
C. The falcon prevents the king from drinking the poison.
D. The king causes the death of the falcon.

____ 11. As a folk-tale character, what are the two main traits that the falcon displays?
A. enthusiasm and impulsiveness
B. resourcefulness and loyalty
C. love of freedom and devotion to duty
D. cleverness and deceit

____ 12. What are King Sindbad's chief character traits?
A. He is harsh and impetuous.
B. He is weak and wavering.
C. He is skilled and clever.
D. He is pious and devout.

____ 13. What do the fisherman, Duban the doctor, and the falcon have in common?
A. All three receive a just reward from a grateful king.
B. All three outsmart people more powerful than they.
C. All three are killed by someone whose life they have saved.
D. All three do not receive the gratitude they deserve.

____ 14. Which of these events is a supernatural element of one of the three folk tales?
A. the doctor's cure for King Yunan's leprosy
B. the vizier's destruction of the doctor's reputation
C. a falcon trained to hunt
D. a snake's venom that gets into King Sindbad's water

____

Name ______________________ Date ______________

15. Which of these is the chief aim of folk tales like "The Fisherman and the Jinnee"?
   A. to amuse the educated upper class
   B. to teach religious doctrine
   C. to entertain the common people
   D. to record the accomplishments of kings and queens

Vocabulary and Grammar

____ 16. Which statement is the most *ominous?*
   A. "I am a jinnee with no use for Allah!"
   B. "You have cured me of a dire disease."
   C. "Evil threatens you, O noble king."
   D. "The king has a-hunting gone."

____ 17. Which word best completes this sentence?
   "And with this cruelty you repay my kindness?" asked the doctor__________
   A. enraptured
   B. indignantly
   C. resolutely
   D. adjured

____ 18. In which sentence is the verb a linking verb?
   A. The fisherman inverted the bottle.
   B. A jinnee jumped out.
   C. He seemed angry and mean.
   D. He threatened the fisherman with violence.

____ 19. In which sentence is the verb an action verb?
   A. The king looked in the doctor's book.
   B. Nothing smelled suspicious to him.
   C. The king felt ill.
   D. The vizier seemed sincere.

____ 20. How can you often tell if a verb is a linking verb?
   A. See whether it can be used with a helping verb.
   B. See whether *-ed* is added to it to form the past tense.
   C. See whether a conjunction such as *and* appears somewhere in the sentence.
   D. See whether it can be replaced with a form of *be* without substantially changing the meaning of the sentence.

Essay

21. Write a summary of "The Tale of King Yunan and Duban the Doctor." Include just the main points and the key details.

22. Choose one of the three tales contained in "The Fisherman and the Jinnee," and write a brief essay explaining how it displays the characteristics of a folk tale. Discuss at least three elements of folk tales that the story displays.

23. Write an essay examining the theme or message that the three folk tales in "The Fisherman and the Jinnee" have in common. Discuss which characters are alike and how their situations and the outcomes of those situations point to the theme.

Name ______________________________ Date ______________

Unit 1: Origins and Traditions
Benchmark Test 1

MULTIPLE CHOICE

Literary Analysis and Reading Skills *Read the selection. Then, answer the questions that follow.*

Tell me, O muse, of Odysseus, that ingenious hero who traveled far and wide after he had sacked the famous town of Troy. Many cities did he visit, and many were the nations with whose manners and customs he was acquainted; moreover, he suffered much by sea while trying to save his own life and bring his men safely home; but do what he might, he could not save his men, for they perished through their own sheer folly in eating the cattle of the Sun-god Helios, so the god prevented them from ever reaching home. Tell me, . . . O daughter of Zeus . . .

from the *Odyssey* by Homer

1. Which of the following archetypal hero's quests is exemplified in this passage?
   A. an extraordinary person goes on a difficult journey or mission
   B. a search for a person, place, or object of value
   C. the search for an answer to a problem or puzzling question
   D. a pursuit of secret spiritual knowledge

2. Which of the following literary techniques is most clearly exemplified in the following phrases from the passage?

   Tell me, O muse, of Odysseus . . . Tell me, . . . O daughter of Zeus . . .

   A. imagery
   B. folk tales
   C. parallelism
   D. archetypal setting

3. Which of the following is a cultural context of ancient Greece that is evident in the passage?
   A. belief in one god
   B. opposition to war as a means of settling disputes
   C. belief in divine intervention in human affairs
   D. belief in the complete responsibility of humans for their fate

4. Which of the following would a reader need to do to summarize the passage?
   A. understand Odysseus' strength as a military leader
   B. understand how the details support a general statement about the passage
   C. understand how the Greeks used muses to help them write
   D. understand what might happen next in the action

Name ______________________________ Date ______________

Read the selection. Then, answer the questions that follow.

Before this Earth existed, there was only water. It stretched as far as one could see, and in that water there were birds and animals swimming around. Far above, in the clouds, there was a Skyland. In that Skyland there was a great and beautiful tree. It had four white roots, which stretched to each of the sacred directions, and from its branches all kinds of fruits and flowers grew.

There was an ancient chief in the Skyland. His young wife was expecting a child, and one night she dreamed that she saw the Great Tree uprooted. The next day she told her husband the story.

He nodded as she finished telling her dream. "My wife," he said, "I am sad that you had this dream. It is clearly a dream of great power and, as is our way, when one has such a powerful dream we must do all we can to make it true. The Great Tree must be uprooted."

from "The Earth on Turtle's Back" retold by Michael J. Caduto and Joseph Bruchac

5. Which of the following can be reasonably inferred about the cultural context from which this passage emerged?
   A. Science played a major role in people's view of the world.
   B. People believed in the ability of dreams to tell the future.
   C. Wives had few rights in marriage.
   D. Water was a scarce and precious resource.
6. Which aspect of an archetypal setting is evident in this passage?
   A. a universe of opposites
   B. a landscape that emerges from watery chaos
   C. a circle that symbolizes completion
   D. a human weakness or sin that sets the gods against the human race
7. Which contrasting images are used in this passage?
   A. roots and branches
   B. clouds and trees
   C. trees and roots
   D. water and swimming
8. In this passage, the Great Tree that connects the realms of heaven and earth is part of which of the following literary elements?
   A. parallelism
   B. imagery
   C. a hero's quest
   D. an archetypal setting
9. Which purpose would a reader most likely have for reading this passage?
   A. to learn more about the true origins of Earth and the universe
   B. to learn about dangers to the natural environment
   C. to learn more about the worldview of ancient Native Americans
   D. to learn about scientific techniques of dream analysis

Name ______________________________ Date ______________

Read the selection. Then, answer the questions that follow.

A powerful monster, living down
In the darkness, growled in pain, impatient
As day after day the music rang
Loud in that hall, the harp's rejoicing
Call and the poet's clear songs, sung
Of the ancient beginnings of us all, shaping
These beautiful plains marked off by oceans,
Then proudly setting the sun and the moon
To glow across the land and light it. . . .

from *Beowulf*, translated
by Burton Raffel

10. How does the monster in this passage correspond to a characteristic of folk tales?
- **A.** The monster teaches a lesson about life.
- **B.** The monster is a magical or supernatural element.
- **C.** The monster is a character that possesses one or two main traits.
- **D.** The monster shows a clear separation between good and evil.

11. Which of the following phrases from the passage is a detail typical of an archetypal setting?
- **A.** "a powerful monster, living down in the darkness"
- **B.** "the ancient beginnings of us all, /shaping/These beautiful plains . . ."
- **C.** "day after day the music rang loud in the hall"
- **D.** "the harp's rejoicing"

12. According to this passage, which of the following was made last in the order of creation?
- **A.** the sun and the moon
- **B.** the oceans
- **C.** the plains
- **D.** the earth

Read the selection. Then, answer the questions that follow.

On the morning of the twelfth day the people washed themselves well. The women dried themselves with yellow cornmeal; the men with white cornmeal. Soon after the ablutions were completed they heard the distant call of the approaching gods. It was shouted, as before, four times—nearer and louder at each repetition—and, after the fourth call, the gods appeared. Blue Body and Black Body each carried a sacred buckskin. White Body carried two ears of corn, one yellow, one white, each covered at the end completely with grains.

The gods laid one buckskin on the ground with the head to the west: on this they placed the two ears of corn, with their tips to the east . . .

from "The Navajo Origin Legend" retold by Washington Matthews

Name ______________________________ Date ______________

13. In this passage, when do the gods appear?
   A. immediately after the women dry themselves with yellow cornmeal
   B. immediately after the men dry themselves with white cornmeal
   C. immediately after the completion of all the ablutions
   D. immediately after the fourth call

14. Based on the context clues in this passage, which of the following does the word *ablutions* relate to?
   A. bathing
   B. farming
   C. dancing
   D. warfare

15. This passage comes from a selection titled "The Navajo Origin Legend." What purpose would a reader most likely have for reading the passage?
   A. learning about Navajo war strategy
   B. learning about Navajo family relationships
   C. learning about Navajo farming techniques
   D. learning about Navajo religious beliefs

16. Which of the following is the best summary of the passage?
   A. The Navajo washed every twelve days.
   B. The Navajo used corn only for religious ceremonies.
   C. The Navajo were obedient to their gods.
   D. The Navajo men were more powerful than the women.

Vocabulary

17. Based on your knowledge of the prefix *sub-*, what is the meaning *of subterranean* in the following sentence?

   Subterranean forms of work like mining can be dangerous.

   A. boring
   B. fascinating
   C. underground
   D. airborne

18. Which of the following best defines *commensurate* in the following sentence, based on your knowledge of the meaning of the prefix *com-*?

   The contractor had agreed to take on the huge construction project, because the payment was commensurate with the amount of work involved.

   A. paid in installments
   B. prompt
   C. much more than
   D. equal in measure or size

19. Based on your knowledge of *ab-*, what is the meaning of *abhorrent* in the following sentence?

The most abhorrent aspect of war is the vast waste of human life.

A. hateful
B. necessary
C. excusable
D. frantic

20. Based on your knowledge of the Anglo-Saxon root *-stead-*, what is the meaning of the word *steadfast* in the following sentence?

The soldiers were reassured by their sergeant's steadfast professionalism under enemy fire.

A. questionable
B. invisible
C. firm
D. unsteady

21. What is the likely meaning of *abject* in the following sentence, based on your knowledge of the prefix *ab-*?

The victims of the hurricane were left in abject misery.

A. full of hope
B. showing great pride
C. temporary
D. showing utter hopelessness

22. Based on your knowledge of the Latin root *-vert-*, which of the following best defines the word *revert* in the following sentence?

After improving his grades in the first semester, he began to revert to his irresponsible ways.

A. invent
B. imitate
C. go back
D. move ahead

Grammar

23. Identify the linking verb in the following sentence.

We were all extremely relieved when we received the news that Fluffy, our cat, was going to make a full recovery.

A. were
B. received
C. was going
D. to make

Name ______________________ Date ______________

24. Which of the following sentences is punctuated correctly?
    A. "Pardon me, ma'am," the state trooper said, but do you realize how fast you were going?
    B. "Pardon me, ma'am," the state trooper said, "but do you realize how fast you were going?"
    C. "Pardon me, ma'am" the state trooper said, "but do you realize how fast you were going?"
    D. "Pardon me, ma'am," the state trooper said "but do you realize how fast you weregoing?"

25. Which of the following sentences contains an error in usage?
    A. She stepped into the room very quietly.
    B. It was her favorite room in the whole world.
    C. Once in the room, she lay down on the bed and slipped into a daydream.
    D. She told the child that she would be available into a moment.

26. Which of the following sentences contains a compound predicate?
    A. Serena questioned the advisability of walking all the way to the movie theater.
    B. Serena believed that the theater was so far that she and her friends would not make it in time.
    C. Serena's friends were confident, however, insisting that the walk would be good exercise.
    D. Nevertheless, Serena pleaded and begged and protested until she got her way.

27. Which of the following is true of a compound predicate?
    A. It contains only one verb.
    B. At least two verbs have the same subject.
    C. Each verb has a different subject.
    D. The subject of the sentence is understood but not stated outright.

28. Which of the following is an example of parallelism?
    A. In your accusations, sir, one finds not an iota of truth, honor, or decency.
    B. The nutritionist spoke about the importance of a balanced diet, and a chart of the major food groups was displayed by her.
    C. My grandparents always stressed the importance of diligence and being kind.
    D. Nowadays, you might find a family spending a weekend wandering through the mall instead of seeing them take a drive in the country.

ESSAY

29. Provide an extended definition of what heroism means in modern society. Then, compare and contrast the nature of the quest of one contemporary action hero (from movies, television, or literature) with the heroic quest of a hero from ancient literature.

30. Choose a passage from the Bible—it could be from the Book of Ruth or any other section of your choice—and write a response to this biblical narrative, focusing on the degree to which the biblical passage does or does not provide useful guidelines about personal behavior for a person in modern society.

31. Choose a movie, novel, play, or short story and write a critique of the work, explaining why you think the work does or does not merit the attention of others. Explain which elements of the work—plot, characterization, theme, and so on—work or do not work, and give specific reasons for your opinions.

Name ______________________________ Date ______________

Unit 1: Origins and Traditions

Diagnostic Test 2

MULTIPLE CHOICE

Read the selection. Then, answer the questions that follow.

The term "the media" refers to all of the information and entertainment sources that are available to us, such as radio, television, newspapers, magazines, movies, and the Internet. The term "mass media" became popular in the 1920s, when radio stations began broadcasting nationally, and mass-circulation magazines and newspapers were sold throughout the nation.

By the end of the twentieth century, more than two-thirds of Americans were using the Internet as a major media source. Some critics suggest that information on the Internet is inferior to published material because it is not always checked and edited carefully.

Other observers believe that the media has had a negative influence on our social lives. They fear that watching television may replace strong interpersonal connections and that people with no strong social ties may be more easily influenced by some of the media's more manipulative uses, such as advertising.

Remember that media is almost never neutral—most information sources have a bias or a particular point of view. Be an active reader: read, watch, and browse carefully in order to identify how a given writer wants you to react.

Don't let your media consumption have a negative affect on the relationships you've built with family and friends. Take note of any changes in your behavior that you might be able to attribute to an over-reliance on media, such as an unwillingness to cooperate when working with others. Things such as strengthening your social connections, and maintaining strong listening and speaking skills, will sharpen your ability to question the information presented by the media.

1. Which of the following would be classified as part of the mass media?
   A. an e-mail from a friend
   B. a video from a family vacation
   C. a newspaper's Web site
   D. a business letter
2. The Internet is considered part of the media because it is used
   A. by two-thirds of Americans.
   B. by people all over the world.
   C. to conduct business.
   D. for information and entertainment.
3. In the phrase "mass media," which of the following meanings does the word *mass* have?
   A. quantity of matter
   B. widely circulated
   C. large number
   D. religious service
4. According to the writer of this passage, why should you carefully evaluate information you find on the Internet?
   A. You can find conflicting facts and opinions on the Internet.
   B. The Internet is filled with biased Web sites.
   C. Not all information found on the Internet is carefully checked and edited.
   D. Information found on the Internet is totally reliable.

Name ______________________ Date ______________

5. Some media critics believe that people who spend all their time surfing the net are a victim of this negative influence of the media:
   A. preventing them from making social contacts.
   B. making them so knowledgeable that peers make fun of them.
   C. limiting the areas of information that they are willing to explore.
   D. exposing them to a confusing range of ideas and opinions.

6. According to this passage, an active reader and viewer is someone who
   A. reads many books and goes to a lot of movies.
   B. questions how the media want him or her to react.
   C. participates in many extra-curricular activities.
   D. reads a daily newspaper and watches news on television.

7. This passage asserts that people should try to determine a media source's
   A. main ideas.
   B. supporting details.
   C. audience.
   D. bias.

8. According to the passage, which of the following is most important?
   A. advanced computer skills
   B. curiosity and independence
   C. strong social contacts
   D. a healthy diet and exercise

Read the selection. Then, answer the questions that follow.

An oral history can help you preserve your family's unique history, creating a priceless inheritance that can be passed down from one generation to the next. All you need to get started is an audio or video recorder and some family members to interview.

Prepare for your interviews by compiling a list of questions for your interviewees, or talking points to guide your conversation. Useful topics for discussion include personal achievements, goals, memorable holidays and vacations, and the birth of children.

Begin the interviews with a clear introduction in which each person clearly states their name, date of birth, and where they live. Encourage people to converse naturally, in a clear voice. Gather as many details as possible by asking follow-up questions, but be careful not to interrupt your interviewees. If you are using a video recorder, simply set it up and let it run. You do not need to use fancy cinematic techniques; a steady picture will focus more effectively on the speaker and the stories being told.

9. Which of the following will best help you prepare to interview your family members?
   A. compiling a list of questions or talking points
   B. sharpening several pencils
   C. brewing some coffee
   D. looking through family photo albums

10. The purpose of compiling an oral family history is to
   A. get to know your family better.
   B. preserve information about the family and its members.
   C. contact relatives you have never met.
   D. practice interviewing and videotaping skills.

Name ______________________________ Date ______________

11. What kind of basic information should you get from each family member?
   A. height, weight, and blood type
   B. names of children
   C. favorite color
   D. name, date of birth, and where he or she lives

12. Which organizational pattern is used in the passage?
   A. chronological order
   B. spatial order
   C. cause-effect order
   D. order of importance

13. You are interviewing your elderly Aunt May for your family's oral history. Which of the following questions is the *least* relevant?
   A. Please tell me about your first job.
   B. What do you remember most about growing up on the farm in Kansas?
   C. How did you vote in the last presidential election, and why?
   D. How did you first meet Uncle Alan?

14. If you are using a video camera, why should you avoid fancy cinematic techniques such as zooming in and out and panning across the room?
   A. You want to distract the interviewee from what he or she is saying.
   B. You want to distract the viewer from what he or she is hearing.
   C. You want to make the interviewee look as attractive as possible.
   D. You want to stay focused on the interviewee's face and facial expressions.

15. You are interviewing your Uncle Ted, who has just completed his first Boston Marathon. Which of the following is the best question to ask him *first*?
   A. What did you eat after you finished the Boston Marathon?
   B. What were your favorite subjects in school?
   C. How did you first get interested in running?
   D. How did you feel as you crossed the finish line?

from the **Rubaiyat** by Omar Khayyam
from the **Gulistan** by Sa'di

Vocabulary Warm-up Word Lists

Study these words from the selections. Then, complete the activities.

Word List A

assailing [uh SAYL ing] *v.* attacking; assaulting
The knights were assailing the castle, attacking it from all sides.

beneficent [buh NEF uh suhnt] *adj.* kind
We thought he was kind because he had a beneficent smile.

destined [DES tind] *v.* determined beforehand; fated
Because of her musical ability, Carol thought she was destined to be a concert pianist.

diminished [di MIN isht] *v.* made smaller; decreased
The old woman could not see well after her sight diminished.

enthusiastically [in thoo zee AS tik lee] *adv.* in an excited manner; eagerly
Joe cheered enthusiastically for his favorite football team.

mystics [MIS tiks] *n.* spiritual people; people who believe in truths beyond words
The mystics meditated each morning in the public park.

oppression [uh PRESH uhn] *n.* the act of weighing down; persecution
The king's oppression of his subjects led them to stop paying taxes.

whilst [hwylst] *conj.* during the same time that
The robber entered our house whilst we slept.

Word List B

calamity [kuh LAM uh tee] *n.* disaster; an event full of terrible loss
The earthquake was a calamity that caused many deaths and much destruction.

consequence [KAHN suh kwens] *n.* effect; result
One consequence of Jack's rudeness was that no one asked him to come to the next game.

dispersed [di SPERST] *v.* broke up; scattered in many directions
The police dispersed the crowd that had gathered around the accident.

pacified [PAS uh fyd] *v.* eased the anger of; calmed
The mother pacified her crying baby by giving him a toy.

prosperity [prah SPER uh tee] *n.* the state of having financial security; success
The man's prosperity enabled him to live in a large mansion.

oneself [wuhn SELF] *n.* a person's own self
One should dress oneself in a costume for a costume party.

oppress [uh PRES] *v.* weigh down; persecute
The bully would oppress his smaller schoolmate each day at recess.

whereas [hwer AZ] *conj.* while at the same time
I like to eat chocolate, whereas you enjoy fresh fruit.

Name ______________________ Date ____________

from the **Rubaiyat** by Omar Khayyam
from the **Gulistan** by Sa'di

Vocabulary Warm-up Exercises

Exercise A *Fill in each blank below with the appropriate word from Word List A.*

Because he believed that he was [1] ______________ to do something important, Charles decided to travel around the world in search of a purpose. When he visited Turkey, he watched Sufi [2] ______________ perform their famous dance. [3] ______________ he toured Italy, he walked among ancient Roman ruins. Charles clapped [4] ______________ for his favorite singer during a performance at a German opera house. However, his excitement for traveling [5] ______________ when he visited Sudan. He saw that the terrible tragedies [6] ______________ that country were war and hunger. Charles also wondered whether the Sudanese people suffered [7] ______________ under the rule of the current government. He decided that he would appeal to wealthier people's [8] ______________ natures in an effort to persuade them to donate necessary supplies for the Sudanese.

Exercise B *Answer the questions with complete explanations.*

1. If someone hurt you, would you be pacified if he or she offered you an apology? Explain your answer.

   ____

2. Which is more important to you: prosperity or happiness? Explain.

   ____

3. What is a consequence of lying to your best friend? Explain.

   ____

4. If you dispersed flower seeds in the ground, what is likely to happen?

   ____

5. Explain why it is important to keep oneself healthy.

   ____

6. You like to eat salad, whereas your friend likes to eat sandwiches. Where should you meet for lunch?

   ____

7. Name one type of weather that is capable of causing a calamity.

   ____

8. Explain how you would deal with a person who tries to oppress you.

   ____

Name ______________________ Date ______________

***from the* Rubaiyat** by Omar Khayyam
***from the* Gulistan** by Sa'di

Reading Warm-up A

Read the following passage. Pay special attention to the underlined words. Then, read it again, and complete the activities. Use a separate sheet of paper for your written answers.

The Seljuk Turks are named for a tribal chief of the same name. Although they began as a tribe, they were destined to rule an empire in Central Asia and the Middle East. During their quest for territory, Chief Seljuk's grandson, Togrul, led the Seljuks into Persia. They fought and conquered various tribes in this area. In 1055, they gained control of much of the region that is now known as Iran. They declared that the Iranian city of Isfahan was their capital.

The Seljuks developed an efficient government in this area. It used able administrators from this region as well as from other areas. However, the Iranian peoples resented their Seljuk rulers. Whilst they were in power, the Seljuks used military force to control their subjects. This military force resulted in the deaths of many people. The Seljuks also forced their subjects to convert to a form of Islam that did not include mystics.

The Seljuks' oppression of the Iranian peoples proved to be disastrous. Because of this persecution, support for the Seljuk leaders quickly diminished. Many Iranians organized themselves to overthrow the Seljuks. They worked enthusiastically to persuade other Iranians to join their cause. Their excitement about their cause won them many allies from different Iranian ethnic groups. They eventually succeeded by assailing the Seljuks, driving them out of Iran.

The Seljuk government began to break down during the twelfth century. In 1153, the last Seljuk ruler demanded that a group of tribespeople pay taxes. The people refused, and instead, they captured the ruler. However, the tribespeople were beneficent to him. Although they kept him prisoner for three years, he was treated with the respect that a ruler deserves. By the thirteenth century, the Seljuks had lost control over many of the regions they had conquered.

1. Underline the phrase that tells what the Seljuks were destined to achieve. Tell what ***destined*** means.
2. Underline the phrases that tell what the Seljuks did whilst they were in power. Use ***whilst*** in a sentence.
3. Were mystics a part of the form of Islam practiced by the Seljuks? Tell what ***mystics*** means.
4. Underline the phrases that tell what oppression means. Use ***oppression*** in a sentence.
5. Underline the sentence that shows that support for the Seljuk leaders diminished. Tell what ***diminished*** means.
6. Underline the phrase that is a clue to the meaning of enthusiastically. Use ***enthusiastically*** in a sentence.
7. Circle the phrase that tells what result the Iranians achieved by assailing the Seljuks. Tell what ***assailing*** means.
8. Underline the phrase that describes the beneficent treatment given to the captured Seljuk ruler. Tell what ***beneficent*** means.

Name ______________________________ Date ______________

***from the* Rubaiyat** by Omar Khayyam
***from the* Gulistan** by Sa'di

Reading Warm-up B

Read the following passage. Pay special attention to the underlined words. Then, read it again, and complete the activities. Use a separate sheet of paper for your written answers.

Sufism is a form of Islamic mysticism that has been practiced for centuries. Sufism originated in the Middle East; however, many people around the world practice Sufism today. People who practice Sufism look for the truth about divine love through direct personal experience with God. They believe that nothing should stand in the way of this experience. They study the Qur'an and the histories of the lives of important Muslims, such as Muhammed.

Sufis' desires for fulfillment are not pacified, or calmed, by obtaining material things. Sufis are not interested in achieving wealth or prosperity. Instead, they seek to become closer to God through love and voluntary suffering.

Whereas some religions are based on logic, the Sufi mystics think that a person needs knowledge that comes from inspiration. They believe that one obtains this inspiration by subjecting oneself to various disciplines. These disciplines include performing meditation and living in poverty. One order of Sufis, the whirling dervishes, believes that inspiration is obtained through the performance of a special dance. The Sufi mystics believe that they will grow closer to God as a consequence of these activities.

The Sufis are also known for their traditional literature. The Sufi poetry of Rumi, Hafiz, Omar Khayyam, and Yunus Emre is still popular. It has been dispersed among various peoples all over the world. The poetry deals with various subjects, including love.

Throughout history, various peoples and rulers have attempted to oppress the Sufis and stop them from practicing their religion. However, these attempts were not successful, and a cultural calamity was avoided.

Today, many people realize that Sufism has influenced large parts of the Muslim world through its philosophy and literature. Other people simply appreciate Sufi literature for its beauty; they value the cultural and artistic contributions that Sufism has made to the world.

1. Underline the word that is a clue to the meaning of pacified. Use ***pacified*** in a sentence.
2. Explain why the Sufis are not interested in achieving prosperity. Tell what ***prosperity*** means.
3. Underline the two contrasting ideas that the word whereas connects. Use ***whereas*** in a sentence.
4. Circle the words that explain what "one" subjects "oneself" to. Use ***oneself*** in a sentence.
5. Underline the phrase that explains the consequence of meditation and living in poverty for Sufi mystics. Tell what ***consequence*** means.
6. Circle the phrase that is a clue to the meaning of dispersed. Use ***dispersed*** in a sentence.
7. Underline the phrase that helps to explain what oppress means. Use ***oppress*** in a sentence.
8. Circle the word that tells what kind of calamity was avoided. Tell what ***calamity*** means.

Name ______________________ Date ______________

from **The Rubáiyát** by Omar Khayyám

from the **Gulistan:** *from* **"The Manners of Kings"** by Sa'di

Literary Analysis: Didactic Literature

Didactic literature teaches lessons about ethics, or the principles of determining right conduct from wrong. Tools of didactic literature include aphorisms (short sayings), personification (a figure of speech giving human qualities to an animal or object), and metaphor (a figure of speech equating two unlike things). Didactic literature communicates lessons about how we should behave by condensing a lesson into an easy-to-remember expression or a memorable story.

Below you will find a passage that represents each of the tools of didactic literature: an aphorism from the *Gulistan*, personification from the *Rubáiyát*, and metaphor from the *Rubáiyát*. For each passage, state in your own words the lesson it teaches and how it applies to your own experience or some aspect of present-day life.

A. Aphorism: A tyrannic man cannot be a sultan / As a wolf cannot be a shepherd.

Lesson that it teaches about life:

____

____

How it applies to my experience or present-day life:

____

____

B. Personification: Wake! For the Sun, who scatter'd into flight / The Stars before him from the Field of Night, / Drives Night along with them from Heav'n, and strikes / The Sultán's Turret with a Shaft of Light.

Lesson that it teaches about life:

____

____

How it applies to my experience or present-day life:

____

____

C. Metaphor: The Moving Finger writes; and, having writ, / Moves on: nor all your Piety nor Wit / Shall lure it back to cancel half a Line, / Nor all your Tears wash out a Word of it.

Lesson that it teaches about life:

____

____

How it applies to my experience or present-day life:

____

____

Name ______________________________ Date ______________

from **The Rubáiyát** by Omar Khayyám

***from the* Gulistan: *from* "The Manners of Kings"** by Sa'di

Reading Strategy: Break Down Long Sentences

In order to understand a lengthy sentence, you should **break down the sentence** into its key parts. Who or what is performing the action? What is being done? Does the sentence describe several actions? Separate the basic elements from the difficult language to boil down the sentence to its main idea.

DIRECTIONS: *Break down the following sentences into their key parts. Underline the doer of each action once, and underline each action (including the receiver of the action) twice. Draw a vertical line to separate groups of doers and actions from one another. Then, rephrase the sentence in your own words.*

1. "The helpless fellow began to insult the king on that occasion of despair, with the tongue he had, and to use foul expressions according to the saying: *Who washes his hands of life / Says whatever he has in his heart.*" —Sa'di, from "The Manners of Kings"

   ____

   ____

   ____

2. "The Worldly Hope men set their Hearts upon / Turns Ashes—or it prospers; and anon, / Like Snow upon the Desert's dusty Face, / Lighting a little hour or two—is gone." —Omar Khayyám, the *Rubáiyát*, XVI

   ____

   ____

   ____

3. "The vizier asked the king how it came to pass that Feridun, who possessed neither treasure nor land nor a retinue, established himself upon the throne." —Sa'di, from "The Manners of Kings"

   ____

   ____

   ____

Name ______________________________ Date ______________

from **The Rubáiyát** by Omar Khayyám
from the **Gulistan:** *from* **"The Manners of Kings"** by Sa'di

Vocabulary Builder

Using the Latin Root *-tort-*

The Latin root *-tort-* means "twist." A *tortuous* path is one with many twists and turns. To *distort* something means to twist it out of its correct shape, figuratively.

A. Directions: *List as many words as you can think of that include the root -tort- plus the prefixes and suffixes in the box. (You will not always need both a prefix and a suffix, but you will usually need one or the other.) Define the words.*

con-	dis-	ex-	re-	-tion	-ous	-ed	-ure	-ist

____

____

Using the Word List

repentance	myriads	beneficent
pomp	piety	extortions

B. Directions: *Complete each sentence with the appropriate Word List word.*

1. The coronation was marked by ____________ and ritual.
2. His rude actions bothered me, but his touching ____________ led me to forgive him.
3. The man's ____________ made him rich for a while but eventually landed him in prison.

C. Directions: *On the line, write the letter of the word that is most nearly the opposite of the italicized word as it is used in the sentence.*

____ 1. The old woman's *piety* brought her to church often.
A. religiousness B. profanity C. terror D. courage

____ 2. He was known to be *beneficent*, and many people applied to him for donations.
A. malicious B. kind C. poor D. sorrowful

____ 3. The *myriads* overwhelmed the organizers, who had expected a low turnout.
A. few B. many C. voters D. protesters

Name ______________________________ Date ______________

***from* The Rubáiyát** by Omar Khayyám

***from the* Gulistan: *from* "The Manners of Kings"** by Sa'di

Grammar and Style: Interjections

An **interjection** is a short expression of emotion that functions independently of a sentence. Writers use interjections to express feelings like surprise, happiness, fear, wonder, scorn, or confusion. Sometimes interjections express very strong emotions, but not always. In some cases, an interjection stands alone, completely outside the sentence, but at other times it is part of the sentence. When an interjection stands alone, particularly if it expresses a strong feeling, punctuate it with an exclamation point.

Wow! I never thought we'd be so lucky.

When an interjection is part of a sentence, it is usually punctuated with a comma.

Ah, how I love the smell of freshly baked cookies.

A. PRACTICE: *Add commas, exclamation points, and periods to correct the punctuation of the items below. Add capital letters where necessary.*

1. Well look at what we have here

   ____

2. Yea our team finished first in the finals

   ____

3. No don't say that

   ____

4. Alas I never reached my goal

   ____

5. Oh my this is so exciting.

   ____

B. Writing Application: Rewrite this passage from the *Rubáiyát* in modern prose or poetry, and including interjections where you can. Use correct punctuation.

A Book of Verses underneath the Bough,
A Jug of Wine, a Loaf of Bread—and Thou
Beside me singing in the Wilderness—
Oh, Wilderness were Paradise enow!

____

____

____

____

____

____

Name ______________________________ Date ______________

***from* The Rubáiyát** by Omar Khayyám

***from the* Gulistan: *from* "The Manners of Kings"** by Sa'di

Support for Writing

Use the chart below to list some ideas for writing your own fable aimed at a modern-day leader or role model. Think of at least two issues with which the leader is involved. Then, move down the chart to jot down notes on the lesson, plot, characters, and character traits that might flow from the issues.

Issues Faced by Present-Day Leaders		
Lesson to Be Learned from the Issues		
Possible Plot Based on Issues		
Characters to Appear in Story		
Characters' Main Flaws and Virtues		

Now, select one of your issue ideas, and use your notes to begin drafting your fable.

Name ________________________________ Date ________________

from **The Rubáiyát** by Omar Khayyám
from the **Gulistan:** *from* **"The Manners of Kings"** by Sa'di

Support for Extend Your Learning

Research and Technology

Use the following chart as an aid in organizing your **annotated anthology** of poems that express the philosophy of life known as *carpe diem*, or "seize the day."

Poem Title	Brief Comment on How the Poem Relates to the Theme of "Seize the Day"

Listening and Speaking

Use the following questions to help you to organize a **panel discussion** about one of the aphorisms, philosophies, or moral lessons presented in the *Rubáiyát*.

1. Which three aphorisms or moral lessons would make the best subject for a panel discussion?
____
____
____

2. Which of the above three items would make the best subject of all? Why?
____

3. How does this aphorism or moral lesson apply to the present-day world?
____

4. If panel members have assigned topics, list topics and assignments.
____
____
____

5. What are the advantages and disadvantages of taking questions from the class?
____
____

Name ______________________ Date ______________

from **The Rubáiyát** by Omar Khayyám
from the **Gulistan:** *from* **"The Manners of Kings"** by Sa'di

Enrichment: World Languages

The *Rubáiyát* by Omar Khayyám is one of the most widely read books of poetry in the world. However, these now-famous verses were scarcely known to Western readers before 1860. In that year, a noted English poet, Dante Gabriel Rossetti, happened upon a pamphlet containing an English translation of Khayyám's poems. Rossetti's praise sparked a booming popularity for this obscure volume.

The translator was a marginal figure in English literature named Edward FitzGerald (1809–1883). FitzGerald published little throughout his life; it was not until he was in his forties that he took up the study of Asian cultures and Persian, the original language of the *Rubáiyát.* Those labors led him to the work of Khayyám, and in 1859 FitzGerald published his pamphlet-sized English translation of the *Rubáiyát.* Within a few years, a private labor of love had become a bestseller and an enduring classic.

Had FitzGerald not taken up the study of Persian, the Western world might have been deprived of some of its loveliest and most memorable verse. Nowadays, knowledge of foreign languages and cultures is far more common among peoples of all nations—increasingly a necessity of the wired "global village" of the twenty-first century, rather than the scholarly pastime it was for FitzGerald back in the 1800s. Thanks to mass media, computers, and rapid transportation, hundreds of millions of people can leap across oceans and national boundaries to make friends, conduct business, and share music, poetry, photographs, and films. It took nearly two thousand years for the *Rubáiyát* to reach Western bookshelves. However, today on the World Wide Web, we can learn about the work of Iranian writers and poets—and those of dozens of other countries—in a matter of seconds.

DIRECTIONS: *Explore the need to know a variety of languages by answering the following questions:*

1. In what specific ways do you think the world has become smaller because of technology and transportation? Do you think the world should have become smaller? Why or why not?

   ____

   ____

2. What products do we import from and export to foreign countries? Why might some people need to know more than one language in today's global economy?

   ____

   ____

3. If people throughout the world could speak a variety of languages, might countries enjoy better relationships? Why or why not?

   ____

   ____

Name ______________________ Date ______________

from The Rubáiyát by Omar Khayyám
from the Gulistan: *from* "The Manners of Kings" by Sa'di
Selection Test A

Critical Reading *Identify the letter of the choice that best answers the question.*

____ 1. What moral or lesson does "Come, fill the Cup . . ." from *The Rubáiyát* suggest?
A. Work hard at your job.
B. Time is on your side.
C. Nature is a mystery.
D. Enjoy your life.

____ 2. In *The Rubáiyát,* the poet says: ". . . the Bird is on the Wing." What life lesson is he offering?
A. There is a life after this one.
B. Time lasts forever.
C. Birds are friends of humans.
D. Life is short.

____ 3. Which sentence would best replace "The Leaves of Life keep falling one by one" from *The Rubáiyát?*
A. We do not appreciate nature enough.
B. We are unable to keep the land clean.
C. We get closer to death each day.
D. We are losing wealth all the time.

____ 4. How else could this long line from *The Rubáiyát* be expressed?
Myself when young did eagerly frequent / Doctor and Saint, and heard great argument . . .
A. I sought wisdom when I was young.
B. I wasted my youth on silly things.
C. I was often ill as a youth.
D. I had trouble with my temper as a youth.

____ 5. Which sentence best expresses the overall lesson of the poems from *The Rubáiyát?*
A. Be good to others in return for kindness.
B. The next world is better than this life.
C. Life is filled with suffering.
D. Enjoy life, for it is brief and precious.

____ 6. Which phrase from *The Rubáiyát* is used to express the idea of fate that controls our lives?
A. "Heart's Desire"
B. "The Moving Finger"
C. "Doctor and Saint"
D. "The Leaves of Life"

____

Name ________________________________ Date ________________

from **The Rubáiyát** by Omar Khayyám

from the **Gulistan:** *from* **"The Manners of Kings"** by Sa'di

Selection Test B

Critical Reading *Identify the letter of the choice that best completes the question.*

____ 1. What is the lesson behind the following lines from *The Rubáiyát*?

How Sultan after Sultan with his Pomp / Abode his destined Hour, and went his way

A. Wealth and position count for nothing after death.
B. Everyone, no matter how important, must die when the time comes.
C. Everyone, even royalty, must stop and rest sometimes.
D. Riches should be enjoyed for as long as possible, for life will end.

____ 2. For what purpose does the speaker of *The Rubáiyát* need the following?

A Book of Verses underneath the Bough,
A Jug of Wine, a Loaf of Bread—and Thou . . .

A. to take advantage of the lovely spring weather
B. to enter paradise
C. to be at peace with his love
D. to enjoy a good lunch

____ 3. The poems from *The Rubáiyát* demonstrate the belief that
A. life is brief but pleasurable.
B. death brings relief from life' s troubles.
C. life is but a stop on the way to Paradise.
D. death is horrible but inevitable.

____ 4. In the selection from "The Manners of Kings," what does the king finally do about the condemned man who has insulted him?
A. He puts him to death.
B. He scolds and then imprisons him.
C. He forgives him.
D. He makes him a vizier.

____ 5. What advice does the following quotation from "The Manners of Kings" represent?

"A falsehood resulting in conciliation is better than a truth producing trouble."

A. Always fight for what is right.
B. Do what is necessary to avoid strife.
C. Avoid those with whom you disagree.
D. Tell the truth no matter whom it hurts.

____ 6. A vizier, one of the characters in the selection from "The Manners of Kings," is
A. a government officer.
B. a slave.
C. a ruler.
D. a religious teacher.

Name ______________________________ Date ________________

____ 7. What lesson does the selection from "The Manners of Kings" teach about the relationship between ruler and subjects?
A. Rulers' power depends on the support of their subjects.
B. A ruler must govern strictly in order to prevent rebellion.
C. Rulers should do only what their subjects want them to do.
D. Rulers with strong armies need not worry about their subjects.

____ 8. Which of the following best expresses the lesson of these lines from *The Rubáiyát*?
Myself when young did eagerly frequent / Doctor and Saint, and heard great argument / About it and about: but evermore / Came out by the same door where in I went.
A. I wasted a good part of my youth in frivolous conversations.
B. I was a sickly youth, and the best minds available couldn't figure out what was wrong with me.
C. In my youth I learned nothing from the most brilliant minds that I consulted.
D. The most brilliant minds I consulted as a youth had no patience for a callow lad me.

____ 9. Breaking down the following passage from *The Rubáiyát* reveals that "a momentary taste of BEING" means which of the following?
A Moment's Halt—a momentary taste / Of BEING from the Well amid the Waste / And Lo!—the phantom Caravan has reach'd / The NOTHING it set out from—Oh, make haste!
A. life
B. death
C. joy
D. sorrow

____ 10. Which best expresses the meaning of the "what boots it" in this passage from the *Gulistan*?
When the pure soul is about to depart, / What boots it if one dies on a throne or on the ground?
A. Who cares?
B. Who knows?
C. What does it matter?
D. What is the reason for it?

____ 11. In tale 7 from the *Gulistan*, what remedy does the philosopher use on the slave who is afraid of traveling on a boat?
A. He administers forty lashes on the slave's back.
B. He diverts his attention from the sea with a long tale.
C. He offers him sympathy and counseling in a calm, reassuring voice.
D. He has him thrown into the sea.

Vocabulary and Grammar

____ 12. Someone who is *beneficent* is likely to treat other people
A. coldly.
B. cruelly.
C. kindly.
D. intelligently.

Name ______________________ Date ______________

____ 13. Which of the following would most likely be a crime?
A. assertions
B. myriad
C. wiles
D. extortions

____ 14. The opposite of *piety* is
A. disrespect
B. despair
C. hatred
D. stupidity

____ 15. Which of the following words would most appropriately modify *assertions*?
A. hungry
B. gentle
C. lonely
D. confident

____ 16. Which of the following lines contains an interjection?
A. "Wake! For the Sun, who scatter'd into flight / The Stars before him . . ."
B. "Come, fill the Cup. . . ."
C. "Ah, take the cash and let the credit go. . . ."
D. "Strange, is it not?"

____ 17. What emotion does the interjection in the following lines help to express?
"O fool, altogether I do not weigh three drachms / How can a pearl of ten drachms be within me?"
A. surprise
B. scorn
C. sadness
D. fear

Essay

18. In the selection from "The Manners of Kings," Sa'di writes,
"A falsehood resulting in conciliation is better than a truth producing trouble."
Do you agree with that point of view? Why or why not? Explain your answer in an essay.

19. A major theme in many works of literature is the fleeting nature of human life. Choose either the selection from *The Rubáiyát* or the selection from "The Manners of Kings," and write an essay in which you discuss the author's view of the brevity of human existence as presented in the selection.

Name ______________________ Date ______________

From the Translator's Desk

Coleman Barks Introduces the Poetry of Rumi

DIRECTIONS: *Use the space provided to answer the questions.*

1. When and how did Coleman Barks first become acquainted with the poetry of Rumi?

2. What did Barks do at the Bluebird Restaurant in downtown Athens, Georgia?

3. How does Barks describe his personal connection to the poetry of Rumi, and how did this connection involve Cappadocia?

4. What does Barks mean by the saying, "I am what I don't know"?

5. According to Barks, what is the difference between the word *springs* and the word *fountain*?

6. How does Barks explain the fact that Rumi is now the most-read poet in the United States?

7. What do you think are some tests or criteria for good poetry? Briefly explain your answer.

Name ______________________ Date ______________________

Coleman Barks

Listening and Viewing

Segment 1: Meet Coleman Barks

- How did Coleman Barks "release" the poems of Rumi "from their cages"?

____

____

____

____

Segment 2: Coleman Barks on Rumi

- Why does Coleman Barks find Rumi's poetry compelling?
- Rumi's poetry is seven hundred years old—why is it still so relevant to today's students?

____

____

____

____

Segment 3: The Writing Process

- How are the voices in Coleman Barks's translation process and writing process different?
- Why do you think it is important for a translator to have two voices?

____

____

____

____

Segment 4: The Rewards of Writing

- Why do you think it is important to create a "global self," as Barks recommends?
- What do you think you could learn by reading a translation, such as the poetry of Rumi?

____

____

____

____

"Elephant in the Dark," "Two Kinds of Intelligence," "The Guest House," and **"Which Is Worth More?"** by Rumi

Vocabulary Warm-up Word Lists

Study these words from the selections. Then, complete the activities.

Word List A

acquired [uh KWYRD] *v.* got; obtained possession of
Nan acquired her knitting skills by taking classes.

conduits [KAHN doo its] *n.* pipes; channels for carrying things, such as fluids
These pipes serve as conduits for the water that flows through them.

depression [di PRESH uhn] *n.* low spirits; the state of being dejected
The elderly man suffered from a mild depression after his dog died.

genuine [JEN yoo in] *adj.* not fake; real
The expert assured Anne that the diamond in her ring was genuine.

grateful [GRAYT fuhl] *adj.* thankful; appreciative
We were grateful to the rescuers for saving us from the sinking ship.

intelligence [in TEL uh juhns] *n.* power of understanding; ability to think and reason
Brain surgeons must possess great intelligence in order to perform their work.

malice [MAL is] *n.* spite; a desire to see others suffer
People will like you more if you treat them with kindness rather than malice.

preserved [pri ZERVD] *v.* protected; kept safe from harm
Sarah preserved all of the letters that Jack sent to her from Paris.

Word List B

awareness [uh WER nis] *n.* state of being informed; consciousness
Your awareness of the issues was clear from your speech.

competence [KAHM puh tuhns] *n.* fitness; ability
Jack demonstrated his competence by completing the project three weeks early.

honorably [AHN er uh blee] *adv.* honestly; with decency or respect
You behaved honorably when you returned the money to its rightful owner.

overflowing [oh ver FLOH ing] *v.* spilling over; flooding
The water in the bathtub was overflowing because Fran forgot to turn off the faucet.

preserving [pri ZERV ing] *v.* maintaining; saving; keeping from harm
Scientists will be preserving the ancient pottery so that future generations may study it.

reality [ree AL uh tee] *n.* state of being actual; truth
Joe's promise to improve his grades became a reality when he earned an A.

solitude [SAHL uh tood] *n.* loneliness; seclusion
John prefers playing his guitar in solitude rather than performing with a band.

stagnate [STAG nayt] *v.* turn unhealthy or unpleasant because of a lack of movement
The water in that puddle will stagnate if it has nowhere to flow.

Name ______________________________ Date ____________________

"Elephant in the Dark," "Two Kinds of Intelligence," "The Guest House," "Which Is Worth More?" by Rumi

Vocabulary Warm-up Exercises

Exercise A *Fill in each blank in the paragraph below with an appropriate word from Word List A. Use each word only once.*

John's stamp collection contained many [1] __________ rare stamps that cannot be replaced. He [2] __________ these stamps through years of hard work. For this reason, John was [3] __________ to Harry because Harry found a way to keep this collection safe. Harry [4] __________ the stamp collection so that light and heat would not harm it. However, John's gratitude quickly turned to [5] __________ when he discovered that the stamps in his collection had been replaced with fakes. He realized too late that Harry was really one of many [6] __________ for a smuggling ring. John fell into a [7] __________ when he discovered that Harry had sold his beloved stamps. John was upset that his [8] __________ in judging people had failed him.

Exercise B *Answer the questions with complete explanations.*

1. Are cartoons based on <u>reality</u>? Explain.

   ____

2. Name one thing that you own that is worth <u>preserving</u>.

   ____

3. If a person cheated on a test, did that person behave <u>honorably</u>? Explain.

   ____

4. What can you do if water is <u>overflowing</u> in the kitchen sink?

   ____

5. Do you prefer to study with a group of friend or to study in <u>solitude</u>?

   ____

6. Will water <u>stagnate</u> if it flows down a river? Explain your answer.

   ____

7. Name one activity in which you exhibit <u>competence</u>.

   ____

8. Is it important to have an <u>awareness</u> of your surroundings when you cross a busy street? Explain.

   ____

Name ______________________________ Date ______________

"Elephant in the Dark," "Two Kinds of Intelligence," "The Guest House," "Which Is Worth More?" by Rumi

Reading Warm-up A

Read the following passage. Pay special attention to the underlined words. Then, read it again, and complete the activities. Use a separate sheet of paper for your written answers.

Rumi was a Persian poet and spiritual leader who lived during the thirteenth century. Although Rumi may be best known for founding the Sufi sect called the whirling dervishes, he was also one of the most popular Islamic poets of this time. In his works, Rumi wrote about many topics, including tolerance, goodness, charity, and awareness through love. In fact, Rumi is still popular. People still read his poetry today, and they appreciate the true, genuine beauty and emotions contained in his works. They find such honesty refreshing.

Rumi's most popular work is called the *Masnavi.* The *Masnavi* is written in poetic form, and it consists of seven books and 24,660 couplets. In this work, Rumi preserved many of the ideas and images in mystical thought that might have been forgotten. Rumi himself has described this work as a work of destruction because it seeks to replace the desire for material things with the desire for spiritual communion. The idea of achieving closeness to God is a central theme in may of Rumi's poems.

The *Masnavi* has acquired a special importance among many Muslim groups. These groups regard the *Masnavi* as one of the conduits leading to later Islamic poetry. The ideas that flow through Rumi's poetry have been used by poets who came after him. Many Muslims are grateful to Rumi because he has also preserved their cultural history in the *Masnavi.* Rumi's work left a permanent mark on later Islamic thought and culture.

Rumi is also famous for writing love poetry about a person's spiritual love of God. He approached this work with real passion and intelligence; as a result, these poems are full of joy and kindness, not gloom and malice. Some readers have asserted that reading Rumi's poetry has lifted them out of depression. They find the beauty of his words to be uplifting and inspiring.

1. Circle the word that means nearly the same as genuine. Use ***genuine*** in a sentence.
2. Underline the phrase that tells what might have happened if the *Masnavi* had not preserved these ideas and images. Tell what ***preserved*** means.
3. Circle the words that tell what the *Masnavi* has acquired. Tell what ***acquired*** means.
4. Underline the phrase that is a clue to the meaning of conduits. Use ***conduits*** in a sentence.
5. Circle the phrase that explains why many Muslims are grateful to Rumi. Then, use ***grateful*** in a sentence.
6. Underline the phrase that tells what Rumi approached with intelligence. Tell what ***intelligence*** means.
7. Underline the word that means the opposite of malice. Use ***malice*** in a sentence.
8. Circle the words that suggest feelings that are the opposite of depression. Tell what ***depression*** means.

Name ______________________ Date ______________

"Elephant in the Dark," "Two Kinds of Intelligence," "The Guest House," "Which Is Worth More?" by Rumi

Reading Warm-up B

Read the following passage. Pay special attention to the underlined words. Then, read it again, and complete the activities. Use a separate sheet of paper for your written answers.

The whirling dervishes are a group of Sufi mystics. This group is also known as the Mevlevi Order, and it was founded by the poet Rumi in the thirteenth century in Turkey. The dervishes are best known for their ability to perform a difficult dance while praying, but this dance is only one component of their spiritual training. The dervishes view themselves mainly as students of constant spiritual learning, and they dedicate their lives to this task.

The whirling dervishes have existed for the past seven centuries. Historically, they have been respected by various Middle Eastern rulers, but their existence almost came to an end in 1925, when the government of Turkey ordered the group to dissolve. A few of the whirling dervishes worked at preserving their tradition, keeping it alive in the solitude of a few isolated areas in the Middle East. Their success in keeping their tradition alive can be seen in Turkey today.

The whirling dervishes exhibit a great competence in performing their dance. The appearance of the dance may seem simple, but in reality, it is very difficult and structured. The dance is held in a special hall called a *tekke*. The dervishes sit in a circle there. They recite poems. Slowly, they rise and begin to dance. They move from east to west. Each dancer moves in a circle by spinning on his right foot. At the same time, the dancer raises the palm of his right hand and keeps the palm of the left hand facing down. The position of the hands stands for giving and taking. The rhythm of the dance does not stagnate; it gets faster, and the dervishes spin faster. In this way, they believe they will gain an awareness of God.

The whirling dervishes of today may perform their dance to overflowing crowds that spill out of the seats into the aisles. The dervishes are honorably regarded by other religious and cultural groups in Turkey. These groups respect the dervishes for their contributions to Turkish art, music, and poetry.

1. Underline the phrase that explains what preserving means. Use ***preserving*** in a sentence.
2. Circle the word that is a clue to the meaning of solitude. Use ***solitude*** in a sentence.
3. Underline the phrase that tells why the dance requires great competence. Name another activity that requires great ***competence***.
4. Underline the word that means the opposite of reality. Name something that shows things not found in ***reality***.
5. Circle the phrase that proves that the dance does not stagnate. Tell what ***stagnate*** means.
6. Circle the phrase that tells what the dervishes do to gain an awareness of God. Describe a situation in which it is important to have ***awareness***.
7. Circle the phrase that is a clue to the meaning of overflowing. Use ***overflowing*** in a sentence.
8. Underline the word that is a clue to the meaning of "honorably regarded." Tell what ***honorably*** means.

Name ______________________________ Date ______________

"Elephant in the Dark," "Two Kinds of Intelligence," "The Guest House,"
and **"Which Is Worth More"** by Rumi

Literary Analysis: Analogy

An **analogy** is an explanation of how two things or ideas are similar. Analogies are usually extended comparisons. In literature, analogies often seek to understand something unfamiliar or mysterious by showing how it is like something familiar.

DIRECTIONS: *Reread the poem, and then answer the questions on the lines provided.*

The Guest House by Rumi, translated by Coleman Barks

This being human is a guest house.
Every morning, a new arrival.
A joy, a depression, a meanness,
some momentary awareness comes
as an unexpected visitor.
Welcome and entertain them all!
Even if they're a crowd of sorrows,
who violently sweep your house
empty of its furniture,
still, treat each guest honorably.
He may be clearing you out
for some new delight.
The dark thought, the shame, the malice,
meet them at the door laughing,
and invite them in.
Be grateful for whoever comes,
because each has been sent
as a guide from beyond.

1. What unfamiliar or mysterious thing is the subject of the analogy in this poem?

____

2. What is the familiar thing to which the unfamiliar thing is likened in the poem?

____

3. How does Rumi's comparison between something unfamiliar and something familiar help in understanding the unfamiliar thing?

____

____

____

____

____

4. Underline words and images in the poem used to support the analogy.

Name ______________________ Date ______________

"Elephant in the Dark," "Two Kinds of Intelligence," "The Guest House,"
and **"Which Is Worth More?"** by Rumi

Reading Strategy: Make Generalizations

Apply the ideas and themes of your reading by making generalizations. A **generalization** is a broad statement that applies to many situations and is supported by details or evidence. As you read, use the details in Rumi's poems to make generalizations about the author's beliefs, philosophy, and main ideas or messages. Test the validity of each generalization by applying it to multiple elements of the poem or to real-life situations.

DIRECTIONS: *As you read the four poems by Rumi in this grouping, make a generalization about the main idea or insight that you find in each poem. As you make each generalization, note the details that support it. Record both the generalizations and the supporting details in the chart below.*

Poem / Generalization	Supporting Details
"Elephant in the Dark"	
"Two Kinds of Intelligence"	
"The Guest House"	
"Which Is Worth More?"	

Name ______________________________ Date ______________

"Elephant in the Dark," "Two Kinds of Intelligence," "The Guest House,"
and **"Which Is Worth More?"** by Rumi

Vocabulary Builder

Using the Latin Prefix *com-* or *con-*

A. DIRECTIONS: *The prefix* con- or com- *comes from a Latin root word meaning "with" or "together." With this information, complete the following sentence by placing the appropriate word in each blank:* combining, complements, communicates.

Rumi's poetry ________________ profound truths by ________________ sound and sense so seamlessly that each word perfectly ________________ every other word.

Using the Word List

competence	conduits	malice	solitude

B. DIRECTIONS: *On each line, write the letter of the word that implies the opposite of the other two.*

____ 1. A. proficiency B. competence C. ineptitude

____ 2. A. contempt B. congeniality C. malice

____ 3. A. pipes B. conduits C. obstructions

____ 4. A. comradeship B. seclusion C. solitude

C. DIRECTIONS: *On each line, write the letter of the word that is most similar in meaning to the one in the Word List.*

____ 1. competence
A. skill B. inadequacy C. concentration D. wisdom

____ 2. conduits
A. riddles B. flights C. channels D. motors

____ 3. malice
A. kindness B. animosity C. strength D. weakness

____ 4. solitude
A. height B. depth C. community D. isolation

Name ______________________________ Date ______________

"Elephant in the Dark," "Two Kinds of Intelligence," "The Guest House," and **"Which Is Worth More?"** by Rumi

Grammar and Style: Agreement and the Indefinite Pronouns *each* and *no one*

The indefinite pronouns *each* and *no one* are always singular. A singular pronoun must always have a singular antecedent (the noun or other pronoun to which the pronoun refers). When used as a subject of a sentence, a singular pronoun always takes a singular verb.

> **Each** of the girls on the softball team **is** training hard at **her** position. (The singular subject, *each*, requires a singular verb, *is;* the singular pronoun, *her,* requires a singular antecedent, *each.*)

> **No one** on the varsity football squad **knows** whether **he** will make the starting lineup. (The singular subject, *no one,* requires a singular verb, *knows*; the singular pronoun, *he,* requires a singular antecedent, *no one.*)

A. Practice: *Complete each sentence by writing the correct verb on the line.*

1. No one here ______________ (have/has) ever seen an elephant.
2. Each of us ______________ (touch/touches) one place.
3. Each one of them ______________ (are/is) a new arrival.
4. Each ______________ (have/has) been sent as a guide from the beyond.
5. No one ______________ (know/knows) which guest might come to your door.

B. Writing Application: *Rewrite the following sentences, correcting all errors in agreement.*

Example: Each of the boys practice their Spanish every day.
Each of the boys practices his Spanish every day.

1. According to Rumi, each of your moods have their value.
2. Rumi believes that no one of us can know the full extent of the truth on their own.
3. No one can be the complete master of their fate.
4. Each person who have sat alone meditating in a room know the value of moments of solitude.
5. Each of you possess an infinite store of wisdom inside if you will only search for it.

Name ______________________________ Date ______________

"Elephant in the Dark," "Two Kinds of Intelligence," "The Guest House,"
and **"Which Is Worth More?"** by Rumi

Support for Writing

Use the following chart to help you with the prewriting stage of your poem based on the style and content of Rumi's works. Try to think of insights, messages, life lessons, and moods that might lead you to a main idea for your poem. From that main idea, try to come up with a central analogy, metaphor, or image to express your idea and make it more vivid and concrete for your readers.

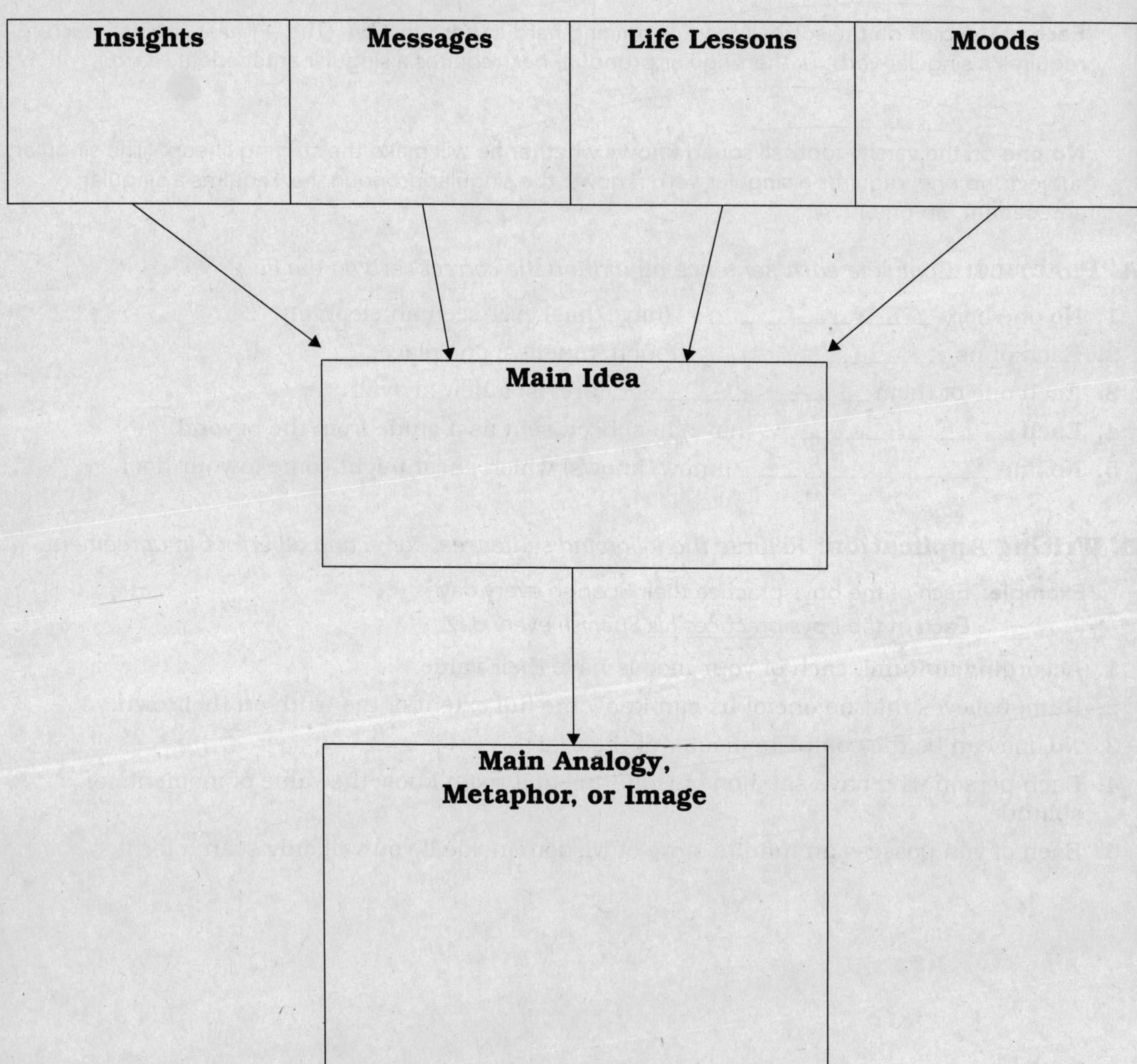

Now, use your notes to begin drafting a poem modeled on the style and content of Rumi's verses.

Name ______________________ Date ______________

"**Elephant in the Dark,**" "**Two Kinds of Intelligence,**" "**The Guest House,**" and "**Which Is Worth More?**" by Rumi

Support for Extend Your Learning

Research and Technology

Use the chart below to organize sources and information for a **research report** on Sufism and whirling dervishes, including the order that Rumi founded.

Sources for Research Report on Rumi/Sufism

Sources for Research Report on Rumi/Sufism
Print or online reference works on Sufism and Rumi: ______________________ ______________________
Internet Web sites about Sufism or Rumi: ______________________ ______________________
Interviews with people who practice Sufism: ______________________ ______________________
Nonfiction books about Sufism or Rumi: ______________________ ______________________

Listening and Speaking

To prepare for your listening session and **group discussion** of recordings of some of Rumi's poems, jot down the answers to these questions.

1. What resources can we use to find cassette or CD recordings of readings of Rumi's poems?
____

2. How much time should we allot for the listening, and how much for the group discussion?
____

3. Should all members of the discussion talk about all aspects of the poems, or should we assign a specific area for each panelist to discuss? ______________________
____

4. What areas should we focus on in our discussion? ______________________
____
____

Name ______________________________ Date ______________

"Elephant in the Dark," "Two Kinds of Intelligence," "The Guest House," and **"Which Is Worth More"** by Rumi

Enrichment: Sufism

The Persian writer Rumi was an adherent of Sufism, the form of Islam that envisions a mystical relationship among human beings, the physical world, and Allah, or God. A mystic is someone who has highly emotional and intense religious experiences filled with wonders and mytery. The word *sufi,* which means "mystic" in Arabic, came from the term *suf,* which means "wool," probably because the early Islamic mystics wore woolen robes. Sufism, which arose around 700, differed from more orthodox Islam in that it sought a personal connection between the believer and Allah, with less emphasis on religious rules and more on emotion. However, this does not mean that Sufis rejected traditional Islam, and in fact most Sufis sought to meld their vision with the rules and doctrines of the religion.

Because Sufis look for evidence of divine truth and wisdom in the physical world, Sufism inspired a great literary flowering, as is evidenced in the work of Rumi. Rumi is believed to have founded the Sufi order known as the whirling dervishes, who seek mystical enlightenment through a wild, spinning dance. Their writings are filled with examples and images that find the presence and wisdom of Allah in the earthly human world.

Directions: *One prevalent image used to envision the presence of divine wisdom is that of light. In the following passage—from another work of Rumi's, "The Marks of the Wise Man, of the Half Wise, and of the Fool"—identify the light images, and explain how they convey the idea of wisdom in the world.*

The wise man is he who possesses a torch of his own;
He is the guide and leader of the caravan.
That leader is his own director and light;
That illuminated one follows his own lead.
He is his own protector; do ye also seek protection
From that light whereon his soul is nourished.
The second, he, namely, who is half wise,
Knows the wise man to be the light of his eyes.
He clings to the wise man like a blind man to his guide,
So as to become possessed of the wise man's sight.
But the fool . . . . has no lamp wherewith to light himself on his way,
Nor half a lamp which might recognize and seek light.

____

____

____

____

Name ______________________________ Date ______________

"Elephant in the Dark," "Two Kinds of Intelligence," "The Guest House,"
and **"Which Is Worth More?"** by Rumi

Selection Test A

Critical Reading *Identify the letter of the choice that best answers the question.*

____ 1. In "Elephant in the Dark," which sense do people use to get an idea of what the elephant looks like?
A. sight
B. hearing
C. touch
D. smell

____ 2. In "Elephant in the Dark," Rumi makes an analogy between how people experience the elephant and which of the following?
A. how people behave toward animals
B. how people treat each other
C. how people experience the world
D. how people make decisions

____ 3. Which statement is a good generalization of the point Rumi is making in "Elephant in the Dark"?
A. No single person knows the entire truth about anything.
B. No one can ever know the truth about anything.
C. It is hard to really know what an elephant looks like.
D. Elephants are confusing animals to understand.

____ 4. What generalization can be made from this passage from "Elephant in the Dark": "If each of us held a candle there, / and if we went in together, / we could see it"?
A. Human cooperation is important.
B. There is a way for blind people to see.
C. Kindness toward elephants is needed.
D. We need to get more light to see better.

____ 5. Which word pair best describes the two kinds of intelligence in "Two Kinds of Intelligence"?
A. what we study and what we teach
B. what we read and what we create
C. what we value and what we feel
D. what we learn and what we are born with

____ 6. How does the metaphor of "a spring overflowing its springbox" describe one kind of intelligence in "Two Kinds of Intelligence"?
A. It is warm.
B. It is lively.
C. It is old-fashioned.
D. It is helpless.

Name ______________________________ Date ______________

___ 7. Which passage from "Two Kinds of Intelligence" is an example of implied metaphor?
A. "There are two kinds of intelligence . . ."
B. "With such intelligence you rise . . ."
C. "a freshness in the center of the chest"
D. "a child in school memorizes facts"

___ 8. What is the poem "The Guest House" about?
A. running a hotel
B. the soul's moods and thoughts
C. traveling around the world
D. proper behavior for guests

___ 9. Which word best describes how the term "guest house" is used in Rumi's poem "The Guest House"?
A. as a metaphor
B. to describe a home
C. in a joking manner
D. as part of a dream

___ 10. Which best expresses the ideas in "Which Is Worth More?"
A. People are happiest with their friends.
B. People feel lonely in a crowd of strangers.
C. Life is lonely for those who rule nations.
D. Freedom and solitude are life's true joys.

Vocabulary and Grammar

___ 11. Which word or phrase is most nearly **opposite** in meaning to the word *malice*?
A. good will
B. ill will
C. cup
D. stamp

___ 12. Which vocabulary word names something that you might find in a room that has electrical wires?
A. competence
B. malice
C. conduit
D. solitude

___ 13. In which situation are you most likely to experience *solitude*?
A. at a restaurant
B. at the movies
C. in a forest
D. in school

Name ______________________ Date ______________

___ 14. Which of the following words is always singular?
A. each
B. all
C. we
D. them

___ 15. Which word best completes the following sentence?
No one in school __________ pleased with the test results.
A. are
B. is
C. am
D. are not

Essay

16. In his poems, Rumi offers advice about different ways to seek truth and wisdom. In an essay, discuss the common thread of advice running through the poems. Use examples from the poems as support.

17. Rumi argues that "genuine solitude" is worth more than "power over an entire nation." Do you agree? Why or why not? In an essay, express your opinion. Support your ideas with examples and reasons.

Name ______________________________ Date ______________

"Elephant in the Dark," "Two Kinds of Intelligence," "The Guest House," and **"Which Is Worth More?"** by Rumi

Selection Test B

Critical Reading *Identify the letter of the choice that best completes the question.*

____ 1. What does "Elephant in the Dark" suggest about how people's opinions are formed?
- A. They are based on thorough research.
- B. They are based on partial knowledge.
- C. They are based on a lack of knowledge.
- D. They are based on the real truth.

____ 2. Which is the best generalization about the view of truth in "Elephant in the Dark"?
- A. Truth can set you free.
- B. Truth has a simple reality.
- C. Truth never changes.
- D. Truth is hard to define.

____ 3. What is the search for truth compared to in the analogy in "Elephant in the Dark"?
- A. group meditation
- B. groping in the dark
- C. a race between contestants
- D. a bright sunny morning

____ 4. What does the person who touches the elephant's tusk think it is?
- A. a candle
- B. an oar
- C. a sword
- D. a tooth

____ 5. Whichgeneralization about human understanding is suggeted by "Elephant in the Dark"?
- A. It leads from the part to the whole.
- B. It leads from the largest to the smallest.
- C. It leads from the top to the bottom.
- D. It leads from the first to the last.

____ 6. The dark room in "Elephant in the Dark" is a metaphor for which of the following?
- A. how humans perceive information
- B. how spiritual leaders gain knowledge
- C. how death takes over everything
- D. how the afterlife can be rewarding

____ 7. In "Elephant in the Dark," how can the image of the dark best be described?
- A. It is an implied metaphor.
- B. It is a direct metaphor.
- C. It is a generalization.
- D. It is a sensation.

Name ______________________ Date ______________

____ 8. Which title is the best generalization of the message of "Elephant in the Dark"?
A. "Overcoming the Fear of Ignorance"
B. "Understanding Ourselves Better By Studying Animals"
C. "Learning to Overcome Our Fears"
D. "Overcoming the Limits of Human Understanding"

____ 9. Which are the kinds of intelligence discussed in "Two Kinds of Intelligence"?
A. learned and inherited
B. artificial and natural
C. partial and whole
D. genuine and fake

____ 10. In "Two Kinds of Intelligence," how does the first kind of intelligence most likely come about?
A. from observing nature
B. from attending classes
C. from meditating in a room
D. from writing a poem

____ 11. In "Two Kinds of Intelligence," people go "in and out of fields of knowledge" to get marks on their "preserving tablets." For which idea is "preserving tablets" a metaphor?
A. understanding of oneself
B. a supply of acquired facts
C. insight into human beings
D. the ability to repair objects

____ 12. Which is true of the second kind of intelligence in "Two Kinds of Intelligence"?
A. It comes from within people.
B. It causes people to be ranked.
C. It is based on book learning.
D. It helps people rise in the world.

____ 13. Which generalization best captures Rumi's message in "The Guest House"?
A. Greet all dark thoughts with strength and courage.
B. A rich imagination can take you on important journeys.
C. Every human being we meet has something to teach us.
D. Even negative experiences can be valuable.

____ 14. In "The Guest House," the guest house is a metaphor for which of the following?
A. the human body
B. the human soul
C. this life
D. the afterlife

____ 15. Which idea guides "Two Kinds of Intelligence," "Which Is Worth More?" and "The Guest House"?
A. seeking wisdom through one's soul
B. shaping one's mind by studying
C. thinking about one's fate in the afterlife
D. respecting the wisdom of older people

Name ________________________________ Date ____________

Vocabulary and Grammar

____ 16. In which location might you feel a strong sense of *malice*?
A. in the playground of a park
B. in the grocery store
C. in a jungle surrounded by angry tigers
D. in a nearby restaurant

____ 17. You would be most likely to find a *conduit* in which of the following items?
A. a plumbing system
B. a heavy book
C. a pencil sharpener
D. a file cabinet

____ 18. Which of the following is most nearly **opposite** in meaning to *competence* ?
A. ability
B. failure
C. fatigue
D. forgiveness

____ 19. Which of the following is true about the word *each*?
A. It is always singular.
B. It is always plural.
C. It is sometimes singular, sometimes plural.
D. It is always a subject of a sentence.

____ 20. Which item in this sentence involves a grammatical error: "No one among Juan's classmates appreciate Rumi more than Ahmad"?
A. No one
B. Juan's classmates
C. appreciate
D. than

Essay

21. Which of the Rumi poems seems to make the best use of metaphor to get its message across? Why? Develop your argument in an essay supported by examples from at least two of the poems.

22. "Elephant in the Dark" notes: "If each of us held a candle there, / and if we went in together, / we could see it." "Which Is Worth More?" says: "A little while alone in your room / will prove more valuable than anything else / that could ever be given you." Do these statements contradict each other? In an essay, discuss the statements and how they do, or do not, relate to each other. Support your response with reasoning and examples.

African Proverbs *from* Sundiata: An Epic of Old Mali

Vocabulary Warm-up Word Lists

Study these words from the selections. Then, complete the activities.

Word List A

enormous [i NAWR muhs] *adj.* very large; immense
Elephants are enormous animals.

experience [ek SPEER ee uhns] *n.* skill or knowledge gained through participation
Joe had experience with emergencies because of his work as a police officer.

foolish [FOOL ish] *adj.* lacking good sense or judgment; silly
It is foolish to criticize something you know nothing about.

journey [JER nee] *n.* a trip
The Gordon family went on a journey to the Amazon jungle.

latter [LAT er] *adj.* the second of two persons or things mentioned
Doctors say that, given a choice between candy and an apple, you should choose the latter.

lively [LYV lee] *adj.* full of energy, activity, or spirit
The students had a lively discussion about their weekend.

memories [MEM uh reez] *n.* recollections; what you remember
We have fond memories of our trip to Paris.

preparations [prep uh RAY shuhnz] *n.* steps you take to get ready for something
The preparations for the exam included reviewing old assignments.

Word List B

buried [BER eed] *v.* hid in the ground; covered from view
The dog buried its bone in the backyard.

capital [KAP i tuhl] *n.* city or town that is the official seat of government
Washington, D.C. is the capital of the United States.

competed [kuhm PEET id] *v.* tried to win something that others are also trying to win
The final two teams competed for the championship trophy.

destiny [DES tuh nee] *n.* fate; inevitable succession of events
The young prince's destiny was to succeed his father as king.

henceforth [hens FAWRTH] *adv.* from now on
Ben was caught speeding yesterday; henceforth, he will not be allowed to drive the car.

likewise [LYK wyz] *adv.* in the same way; also
Mary read the directions; Jeff did likewise, but he still got lost.

mysteries [MIS ter eez] *n.* things that are not fully understood
Television documentaries often deal with unsolved mysteries.

ordinary [AWR din er ee] *adj.* common; usual
Matt did not notice the house on the left because it looked so ordinary.

Name ______________________________ Date ______________

African Proverbs *from* Sundiata: An Epic of Old Mali

Vocabulary Warm-up Exercises

Exercise A *Fill in the blanks, using each word from Word List A only once.*

Jessica has wonderful [1] ________________ of her family's trip to the Grand Canyon. Before she left, she had to make several [2] ________________, including scheduling the flights and packing her clothes. The [3] ________________ to the Grand Canyon was a long one, and the family had to travel by airplane and bus to reach it. When she finally arrived, Jessica was amazed at the [4] ________________ size of the canyon. She and her brother had a [5] ________________ discussion about how it was formed. Even though Jessica's mother and father were both excited to descend into the Grand Canyon, the [6] ________________ became nervous when he saw how long and steep the path was. Eventually, Jessica's father made the trip into the canyon because he did not want to look [7] ________________ or afraid in front of his family. Jessica took many photographs of her trip to the Grand Canyon in order to have a reminder of this unique [8] ________________.

Exercise B *Answer the questions with complete explanations.*

1. If you competed hard against another athlete, what evidence might there be of your effort?
____
2. Is the Empire State Building one of the mysteries of the natural world? Explain.
____
3. If your friend supports a controversial idea and you do likewise, do you agree? Explain.
____
4. Is the Fourth of July an ordinary day in America?
____
5. What event might lead a person to think that his or her destiny is being fulfilled?
____
6. If you've buried your feelings about something, in what way do you express them?
____
7. What government offices does a state capital have that distinguishes it from other cities?
____
8. If you decided that henceforth you would eat right and stay fit, when would you be making these changes?
____

Name ______________________________ Date ______________

African Proverbs *from* Sundiata: An Epic of Old Mali

Reading Warm-up A

Read the following passage. Pay special attention to the underlined words. Then, read it again, and complete the activities. Use a separate sheet of paper for your written answers.

If you like adventure, an African safari might be a truly perfect journey for you. Such a trip can take you into the heart of the African wilderness, where you can closely observe exotic animals, plants, and landscapes. A safari is something that you cannot undertake anywhere else. However, in order to enjoy fully the experience, you need to plan ahead and make several preparations.

A good tour operator can help. However, it is important that you research the operator's qualifications and experience. For example, you may want to know how long the operator has been safely guiding tourists. You may also want to know about the accommodations that these operators offer. Do you want to camp outdoors during your trip, or would you prefer to stay in a hotel? The first option may provide you with an opportunity to see the African wilderness around the clock. The latter may give you a chance to rest more peacefully after a busy day of sightseeing.

The best time to go on a safari is generally in the months of June through August, when the leafy vegetation is not as thick. During this time, many different animals wander in search of food and water, and seeing them tends to be easier.

Remember that you won't be alone. You will probably engage in lively talks about the different types of animals and their habitats with other adventurers. Many people have excitedly reported seeing enormous animals such as elephants, rhinoceroses, and giraffes, so you may want to brush up on your facts.

Finally, you should consider taking some precautions. Because of the strong sunshine in Africa, it would be foolish not to take along a broad-brimmed hat and sunscreen. Bug repellent is also a necessity. When planned carefully, an African safari is a trip designed to make many wonderful memories. It is an exotic travel experience that is like no other.

1. Circle the word that tells what journey means. Describe a ***journey*** you might like to take.

2. Circle the phrase that is a clue to what preparations means. What ***preparations*** might people make at the beginning of the day?

3. What type of experience do you think tour operators should have? Tell what ***experience*** means.

4. Underline the phrase that tells what the latter choice for accommodations could be on a safari. Tell what ***latter*** means.

5. Circle the word that tells what lively means. Use ***lively*** in a sentence.

6. Underline the phrase that lists three of the enormous animals that you may see on a safari. Tell what ***enormous*** means.

7. Underline the phrase that lists what would be foolish to leave behind if you go on a safari. Tell what ***foolish*** means.

8. Underline the phrase that tells why a safari will give you many wonderful memories. Tell what ***memories*** means.

Name ______________________________ Date ______________

African Proverbs *from* Sundiata: An Epic of Old Mali

Reading Warm-up B

Read the following passage. Pay special attention to the underlined words. Then, read it again, and complete the activities. Use a separate sheet of paper for your written answers.

Many people who hear the name "Timbuktu," think of the mysteries of ancient cities lost in the desert, their secrets forever hidden in the shifting sands. In fact, Timbuktu, a city in Mali, Africa, is a real place with a fascinating history and a challenging future.

Located on a trade route that once crossed the Sahara, Timbuktu was a vibrant center for trade in Africa, beginning in the thirteenth century. Likewise, Timbuktu was significant to Muslim scholars as a spiritual capital for Islamic thought and culture during the fifteenth and sixteenth centuries. People came from as far away as Saudi Arabia to study there. As a result, many great mosques, schools, and libraries were built in Timbuktu. To this day, schools for Islamic learning still operate there, and Muslim scholars continue to come to Timbuktu for study.

The golden age of Timbuktu ended in the late sixteenth century, when a Moroccan army destroyed the empire that had built up the African city. Moreover, merchant ships from other areas began trading along the West African coast near Mali, and they competed with Timbuktu for this business. Consequently, Timbuktu declined in importance, and its greatness diminished.

Today, Timbuktu is faced with many problems, but it is by no means an ordinary place. Muslim scholars still go there to study. However, the sand of the Sahara is threatening the city. Blown by the wind, sand is threatening to cover the city and its monuments. The creeping of the Sahara has dried up the water supply, and it has buried many historical buildings. Timbuktu's current destiny of being swallowed up by the desert must be stopped. Henceforth, the goal must be to rescue Timbuktu from the destruction of the sands so that future generations can enjoy its rich history.

1. Underline the phrase that helps explain the meaning of mysteries. What do you think is one of the world's ***mysteries***?
2. Timbuktu was a vibrant center for trade; why was it likewise significant to Muslim scholars? Tell what ***likewise*** means.
3. Underline the phrases that tell how Timbuktu became the spiritual capital for Islamic thought. Tell what ***capital*** means.
4. Underline the phrase that tells what competed with Timbuktu for trade. Tell what ***competed*** means.
5. Underline the phrases that show that Timbuktu is still no ordinary place. Tell what ***ordinary*** means.
6. Underline the phrase that tells what has been buried in Timbuktu. Use ***buried*** in a sentence.
7. Underline the phrase that tells what Timbuktu's current destiny is. Tell what ***destiny*** means.
8. Henceforth, what must be the goal for Timbuktu if it is not to be lost entirely? Tell what ***henceforth*** means.

Name ______________________ Date ______________

African Proverbs
***from* Sundiata: An Epic of Old Mali**

Literary Analysis: Epic Conflict and Proverbs

Conflict in a work of literature may take place in one of three ways: between characters; between a character and an outside force, such as nature or society; or within a character who is torn by opposing desires. In an epic, the hero often endures all three kinds of conflict. It is the hero's ability to overcome such obstacles that marks him or her as heroic.

Proverbs are wise sayings that offer wisdom and guidance for successful living. Like epic poems, they are expressions of particular cultures, reflecting the culture's values and ways of life. Because proverbs provide advice, they often help to resolve conflicts.

A. DIRECTIONS: *Review the excerpt from* Sundiata *in your textbook. Find instances in which Sogolon Djata deals with each of the three kinds of conflict. How does he overcome each obstacle? Write an example of each kind of conflict in the chart, and explain the hero's efforts to resolve it.*

Conflict	Example of Conflict	Resolution of Conflict
1. Between Sogolon Djata and another character		
2. Between Sogolon Djata and society		
3. Within Sogolon Djata		

B. DIRECTIONS: *From the proverbs in this grouping, choose one that is relevant to one of Sogolon Djata's conflicts in* Sundiata. *Write down the proverb, and explain how it applies to Sogolon Djata. Describe how it provides perspective on his situation or helps him solve a conflict. Then, describe how the proverb might be applicable to present-day life.*

Proverb	Application to Sogolon Djata	Application to Present-Day Life

Name ______________________________ Date ______________

African Proverbs

***from* Sundiata: An Epic of Old Mali**

Reading Strategy: Reread for Clarification

Rereading is one of the simplest and most helpful strategies for improving comprehension. For example, when you read a story with a number of names in it, particularly names from a culture you are not familiar with, expect to reread portions to keep the characters' identities straight. If you are reading a passage with a number of actions in it, expect to read it more than once to understand it fully. The meaning of an unfamiliar word usually becomes clear as you reread the context clues that surround it. In addition, rereading an earlier passage may help you make complete sense of a later one.

DIRECTIONS: *Read the following section from* Sundiata. *Answer the questions that follow it, and note the part of the passage you reread in order to answer each question.*

> One day Naré Maghan made Mari Djata come to him and he spoke to the child as one speaks to an adult. "Mari Djata, I am growing old and I shall be no more among you, but before death takes me off I am going to give you the present each king gives his successor. In Mali every prince has his own griot. Doua's father was my father's griot, Doua is mine and the son of Doua, Balla Fasséké here, will be your griot. Be inseparable friends from this day forward. From his mouth you will hear the history of your ancestors, you will learn the art of governing Mali according to the principles which our ancestors have bequeathed to us."

1. Who is speaking? Who is being spoken to? ______________________________

   Quotation reread from the passage: ______________________________

   ____

2. Who was Naré Maghan's father's griot? ______________________________

   Quotation reread from the passage: ______________________________

   ____

3. What is the name of Mari Djata's griot? ______________________________

   Quotation reread from the passage: ______________________________

   ____

4. What will the boy learn from his griot? ______________________________

   ____

   Quotation reread from the passage: ______________________________

   ____

Name ______________________________ Date ______________

African Proverbs
***from* Sundiata: An Epic of Old Mali**

Vocabulary Builder

Using the Latin Root *-firm-*

At the beginning of the excerpt from *Sundiata,* Sogolon is concerned about her son's "infirmity." The word *infirmity* contains the root *-firm-*, which comes from the Latin *firmare,* meaning "to strengthen." Knowing that the prefix *in-* means "lacking" or "without," you can figure out that *infirmity* means "without strength" or "physical weakness."

A. DIRECTIONS: *Complete each sentence with the most appropriate word from the box.*

affirmation	infirmary	confirmation	firmament

1. Students who are not feeling well can rest in the ______________.
2. I called for a(n) ______________ of my Friday appointment.
3. The award was a(n) ______________ of her value as a teacher.
4. There were no clouds interrupting the solid blue ______________.

Using the Word List

fathom	malicious	innuendo	estranged
taciturn	infirmity	diabolical	

B. DIRECTIONS: *Match each word in the left-hand column with its definition in the right-hand column. On the line, write the letter of the definition next to the word it defines.*

___ 1. fathom	A. quiet, aloof
___ 2. taciturn	B. alienated
___ 3. malicious	C. understand; grasp
___ 4. infirmity	D. spiteful
___ 5. innuendo	E. demonic
___ 6. diabolical	F. ailment
___ 7. estranged	G. suggestion; insinuation

C. DIRECTIONS: *Write three sentences, one using each of the following sets of words.*

1. malicious + innuendo + diabolical: ______________________________
2. taciturn + estranged: ______________________________
3. infirmity + fathom: ______________________________

Name ______________________________ Date ______________

African Proverbs
***from* Sundiata: An Epic of Old Mali**

Grammar and Style: Sentence Variety

You can make your writing more interesting and more pleasing to the ear by varying your sentences. There are several ways to achieve **sentence variety.** One way is to use a variety of types of sentences: declarative, interrogative, exclamatory, and imperative.

Declarative: Sologon's son had a slow and difficult childhood.

Interrogative: What three-year-old has not yet taken his first steps?

Exclamatory: How impatient man is!

Imperative: Look as you fell a tree.

Another way to achieve sentence variety is to vary the beginnings of your sentences, as in the following examples.

Sentence Beginning With Adverb: *Often* Sogolon would make some of them come to him to keep him company.

Sentence Beginning With a Prepositional Phrase: *In Mali* every prince has his own griot.

Sentence Beginning With a Participial Phrase: *Having become all-powerful,* Sassouma Bérété persecuted Sogolon because the late Naré Maghan had preferred her.

Sentence Beginning With a Subordinate Clause: *Where there are no dogs,* the cats move about freely.

A. Practice: *Rewrite the following sentences so that each one begins with an adverb, a prepositional phrase, a participial phrase, or a subordinate clause. Underline and identify the type of construction you use.*

1. Sogolon's son could only crawl when he was three years old. ______________

____

2. Sogolon heard gossip about her son and became frustrated. ______________

____

3. Proverbs often find lessons for human behavior in the animal world. ______________

____

B. Writing Application: *On a separate sheet of paper, rewrite the following paragraph, revising it to add sentence variety. Remember that you can add sentence variety by using a combination of declarative, interrogative, and exclamatory sentences and by varying sentence beginnings.*

Sogolon suffered after the death of Naré Maghan. Sassouma Bérété spitefully banished Sogolon and her son to a backyard of the palace. Sogolon was miserable. She wondered whether her son would ever walk. Sogolon Djata promised to walk in order to ease his mother's pain. People were shocked when he kept his promise.

Name ______________________________ Date ______________

African Proverbs
***from* Sundiata: An Epic of Old Mali**

Support for Writing

As you prepare **notes for retelling** a story that you know, you might want to take notes to record useful details about the characters and events that will make up your tale. Use a chart like the one below to jot down these details.

Characters	Character Details
Events	**Event Details**

Now, use your notes to write a vivid, entertaining retelling of a story that you know.

Name ______________________ Date ______________

African Proverbs

from Sundiata: An Epic of Old Mali

Support for Extend Your Learning

Listening and Speaking

Use the questions and lines below to guide your preparation for an **oral retelling** of the selection from *Sundiata.*

1. What are the key details of the story that I should include in my presentation?
____
____
2. What tone of voice should I use for each character? ______________________
____
3. What gestures or movements should I use to re-create various characters and scenes?
____
4. How long should my presentation last? ______________________
5. What questions can I expect from the audience afterward? ______________________
____
____

Research and Technology

Use the chart below to organize the research you will need to do for your **booklet of proverbs.**

Proverb	Country or Region of Origin	Date of Period of Proverb	Source

Name ______________________ Date ______________

African Proverbs
***from* Sundiata. An Epic of Old Mali**

Enrichment: Geography

Sundiata is a legend that for centuries has been shared in what is now the African republic of Mali. Mali is a relatively flat, landlocked country in western Africa. It stretches across three climatic zones: the Sudan, the Sahel, and the Sahara.

The Sudan climate, in southern Mali, is characterized by regular periods of rainfall. It is a fertile area that produces different types of vegetation, including the gnougous, a root vegetable, and the baobab tree mentioned in the selection. Vegetation gradually decreases in the Sahel region, where more drought-resistant types of vegetation grow. In the Sahara, a desert region, vegetation is virtually nonexistent.

DIRECTIONS: *Use the background information above and the map of Mali to answer the following questions.*

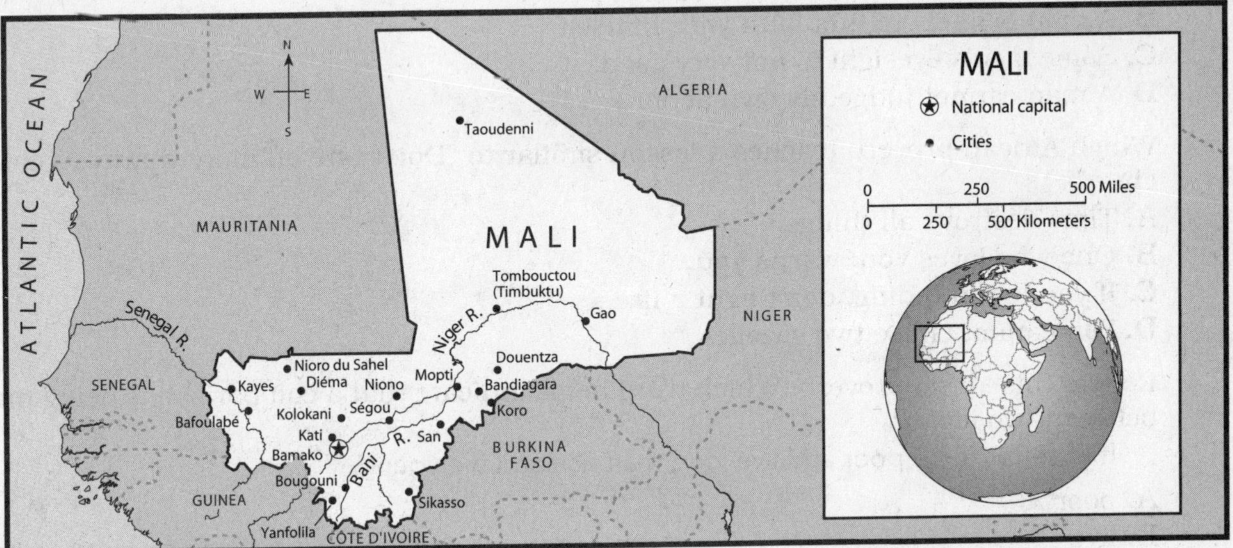

1. In what part of Mali do most people live? Why do you think that is?

____

2. Judging from references in the story to baobab and other types of vegetation, in what climatic zone of Mali did Sogolon Djata probably live?

____

3. What large country borders Mali to the north and east?

____

4. At what city do the Niger River and the Bani River meet?

____

5. What major river runs across the western corner of Mali? What cities lie along this river?

____

Name ______________________ Date ______________

African Proverbs
***from* Sundiata: An Epic of Old Mali**

Selection Test A

Critical Reading *Identify the letter of the choice that best answers the question.*

____ 1. Which word shows the conflict in this Ugandan proverb: "Words are easy, but friendship is difficult"?
- **A.** words
- **B.** easy
- **C.** but
- **D.** difficult

____ 2. Reread this proverb, and select the answer choice that best captures its meaning.

A man's ways are good in his own eyes.

- **A.** Men should be satisfied and not complain.
- **B.** A man is likely to find fault with himself.
- **C.** Some men's eyesight is not very good.
- **D.** A man cannot judge his own actions.

____ 3. Which African proverb teaches a lesson similar to "Don't bite off more than you can chew"?
- **A.** Time destroys all things.
- **B.** One who loves you, warns you.
- **C.** If you are in hiding, don't light a fire.
- **D.** You cannot chase two gazelles.

____ 4. Reread this Masai proverb. Which word helps indicate that a comparison is being made between two ideas?

It is better to be poor and live long than rich and die young.

- **A.** poor
- **B.** live
- **C.** than
- **D.** rich

____ 5. In *Sundiata*, which characteristic of an epic is shown in the contrast between the great future predicted for Sogolon Djata and his inability to walk?
- **A.** menacing enemy
- **B.** moral dilemma
- **C.** difficulty with fate
- **D.** challenging decision

____ 6. Which of these events from *Sundiata* suggests that the character is impatient?
- **A.** Naré Maghan exiles Sogolon and marries another woman.
- **B.** Sogolon Djata tries herbs to cure her child.
- **C.** The queen mother allows people to see the child.
- **D.** The old, blind blacksmith answers the king's question.

Name ______________________________ Date ____________________

____ 7. Which of these would make a good alternative title for *Sundiata*?
A. Born to Rule
B. Jealousy
C. Walking Early
D. The Wisdom of Kings

____ 8. In *Sundiata*, why is Sassouma Bérété so unkind to Sogolon Kedjou?
A. Sogolon is prettier than she.
B. Naré Maghan prefers Sogolon to her.
C. Sogolon insults her.
D. Sassouma's son is not lively.

____ 9. Which character in *Sundiata* is an example of an enemy who menaces Sogolon?
A. Nounfaïri, the blind seer
B. Sassouma Bérété
C. Farakarou, Master of the forges
D. Doua

____ 10. Sogolon Djata's amazing feat at the end of *Sundiata* is an example of which proverb?
A. "How impatient man is."
B. "The silk cotton tree emerges from a tiny seed."
C. "Balla, you will be my griot."
D. "The waters of the Niger . . . cannot wipe out an insult."

____ 11. Reread these passages from *Sundiata*. Which discusses a character's conflict with society?
A. "Mari Djata's mother now occupied an old hut."
B. "Sogolon's son was spoken of with . . . irony and scorn."
C. "The Almighty has his mysteries."
D. "The disheartened king debarred Sogolon from his house."

Vocabulary and Grammar

____ 12. Which character from *Sundiata* could best be described as *malicious*?
A. Naré Maghan
B. Doua
C. Kolonkan
D. Sassouma Bérété

____ 13. Which word is most nearly **opposite** in meaning to *infirmity*?
A. strength
B. illness
C. hunger
D. satisfaction

Name ______________________ Date ____________

____ 14. Which sentence begins with a subordinate clause?
A. Daring talk is not strength.
B. Children are the wisdom of the nation.
C. Eyes do not see all.
D. If you are in hiding, don't light a fire.

____ 15. Which sentence begins with a prepositional phrase?
A. But nothing came of it.
B. Take them then, since your son is unequal to mine.
C. From his mouth you will hear the story of your ancestors.
D. May your destiny be accomplished.

Essay

16. In an essay, compare and contrast one of your favorite heroes with Sogolon Djata of *Sundiata*. How are they alike and different? Develop your ideas in an essay supported by examples and clear reasoning.

17. In an essay, discuss the conflicts faced by Sogolon Djata, the hero of *Sundiata*. Which is the most important? Why? Develop your thoughts in an essay supported by examples from the story.

Name ______________________________ Date ______________

African Proverbs

***from* Sundiata: An Epic of Old Mali**

Selection Test B

Critical Reading *Identify the letter of the choice that best completes the statement or answers the question.*

____ 1. Which word or phrase is most important in establishing the difference between the two behaviors in this proverb?

The one who is hopeful is better off than the one who merely dreams.

A. is hopeful
B. than
C. merely
D. dreams

____ 2. What is the best interpretation of this proverb?

A man who has once been tossed by a buffalo, when he sees a black ox, thinks it's another buffalo.

A. It is good to be afraid of every possible danger.
B. One bad experience may make you overly cautious.
C. Only a fool would mistake a black ox for a buffalo.
D. A black ox is not as dangerous as a buffalo.

____ 3. Which of the following proverbs is most applicable to the story of Sogolon Djata?
A. "Do not say the first thing that comes to your mind."
B. "One falsehood spoils a thousand truths."
C. "Little is better than nothing."
D. "Eyes do not see all."

____ 4. Which words best describe Sassouma Bérété, the king's first wife?
A. kind and honest
B. resentful and vengeful
C. foolish and silly
D. happy and successful

____ 5. Before his death, what present does Naré Maghan give his son Sogolon Djata?
A. a huge iron rod
B. a crown
C. a griot
D. a plot of land

____ 6. When the king asks about Sogolon Djata, what does the soothsayer mean by answering, "Great trees grow slowly but they plunge their roots deep into the ground"?
A. Sogolon Djata will achieve greatness in an incident involving a tree.
B. Although Sogolon Djata is developing slowly, he will someday be a great king.
C. Sogolon Djata will never be king because he is too rooted in the earth.
D. The king has grown to old age and soon will be buried in the ground.

Name ______________________________ Date ______________

____ 7. Why does Sogolon Djata respond calmly when he is tormented?
A. He knows that when the time is right, he will be king.
B. He knows that there is nothing he can do to change public opinion.
C. He feels dispirited and powerless but knows he will be king.
D. He does not like the other villagers, so nothing they say bothers him.

____ 8. Which of these passages best illustrates a conflict between Sogolon Djata and society?
A. "As men have short memories, Sogolon's son was spoken of with nothing but irony and scorn."
B. "Sogolon Kedjou and her children lived on the queen's leftovers, but she kept a little garden in the open ground behind the village."
C. "'Take them then, since your son is unequal to mine.' Then she laughed derisively with that fierce laughter which cuts through your flesh."
D. "'Through your fault I have just suffered the greatest affront of my life! What have I done, God, for you to punish me in this way?'"

____ 9. What effect does the conflict over the baobab leaves have on the story's central conflict?
A. Sogolon Djata decides to threaten Sassouma Bérété for having treated his mother cruelly over the years.
B. Sogolon Djata feels threatened because he sees that the dispute over the baobab tree is meant as a challenge to his right to rule.
C. Distressed by his mother's anguish, Sogolon Djata is moved to ask for the iron bar that will help him stand and get her the baobab.
D. Sogolon Djata goes to the baobab tree to get his mother the leaves she needs.

____ 10. Which was *not* a sign of Sogolon Djata's strength?
A. He brained the other three-year-olds.
B. He picked up the iron bar without effort.
C. He bent the iron bar when he stood.
D. He uprooted a baobab.

____ 11. This excerpt from *Sundiata* is mostly about how Sogolon Djata
A. causes his mother humiliation.
B. at last proves his right to rule.
C. becomes his father's pride and joy.
D. gets revenge against his evil aunt.

Vocabulary and Grammar

____ 12. Which of the following choices best defines *malicious* as it is used in this sentence from *Sundiata*?

Malicious tongues began to blab.

A. optimistic; hopeful
B. threatening; fearful
C. extremely curious
D. intentionally harmful

Name ______________________________ Date ______________

____ 13. Which of the following choices is the best definition of *fathom* as it used in this sentence?

God has mysteries which none can fathom.

A. forget
B. argue about
C. understand
D. appreciate

____ 14. Which of the following is an example of an interrogative sentence?

A. "Sogolon had sat down in front of her hut."
B. "You, perhaps, will be king."
C. "What was he thinking about?"
D. "How impatient man is!"

____ 15. Which of the following sentences uses a different construction from the others?

A. Trying to help her son, Sogolon used rare herbs.
B. The king's first wife rejoiced at Sogolon Djata's problems.
C. Sogolon's son had a difficult childhood.
D. The king and Doua exchanged glances.

____ 16. Which of the following sentences uses a construction different from the others?

A. Sogolon saw her son standing.
B. The smiths had made a great rod.
C. Sogolon wanted baobab leaves.
D. She knew where the baobab was growing.

____ 17. Which of the following proverbs begins with a subordinate clause?

A. Do not say the first thing that comes to your mind.
B. Words are easy, but friendship is difficult.
C. The one who travels is the one who sees things.
D. If you are in hiding, don't light a fire.

Essay

18. Write an essay describing specific conflicts in *Sundiata.* How are these conflicts resolved? How do the conflicts faced by Sogolon Djata make him likely to be a better leader? Support your answer with references to the epic.

19. Choose one of the following African proverbs, and in an essay, explain what it means, what it reveals to you about the culture that created it, and how it might be meaningful to people in our own society.

    One who cannot pick up an ant and wants to pick up an elephant will someday see his folly.
    You cannot chase two gazelles.
    The one who has not made the journey calls it an easy one.
    Rain beats a leopard's skin, but it does not wash out the spots.
    No one tests the depth of a river with both feet.

Name ______________________ Date ______________

Writing About Literature—Unit 1

Analyze Literary Periods

Prewriting: Reviewing the Selections

Take notes about various selections from this unit in the following chart.

Selection	Value	Example	Page #

Drafting: Organizing Logically

Use the following outline to organize your essay logically.

I. Value 1

Selection 1

Selection 2

Selection 3

II. Value 2

Selection 1

Selection 2

Selection 3

III. Value 3

Selection 1

Selection 2

Selection 3

Name ______________________________ Date ______________

Writing About Literature—Unit 1

Analyze Literary Periods: Integrating Grammar Skills

Rephrasing for Clarity

As you revise your essay, make sure that the intended meaning of each sentence is clearly expressed. Reword any sentences that do not clearly express what you mean.

Unclear: Psalm 8 expresses the belief that humans are close to God.

So are angels, but the Psalm expresses the belief that humans are better than other animals.

Clear Psalm 8 expresses the belief that humans are close to God. In their position as God's favorites—just a little lower than the angels—humans rule over the rest of creation.

Revising for Clarity

DIRECTIONS: *Rewrite the following sentences so that their meaning is clear.*

1. Gilgamesh values bravery, loyalty, and heroic deeds. So do other heroes. It's universal.

____

____

2. Gilgamesh searches for eternal life, but he has to deal with death. We all do, because it's part of life.

____

____

3. In a way, a hero like Gilgamesh lives on because people remember.

____

4. The epic of *Gilgamesh* describes a great flood. Other ancient literature does too. It's a common theme: starting over.

____

____

5. Heroes need to keep at it, even when things get rough. Everyone does, really. Gilgamesh shows this.

____

____

Name ______________________ Date ______________

Writing Workshop—Unit 1

Narration: Autobiographical Narrative

Prewriting: Narrowing Your Topic

After choosing the basic topic for your narrative, answer the questions below to help you think about what details you want to include.

What point do you want to make?	
What specific moment will you discuss?	
What people and places will you describe?	
What challenges did you face?	
What life lesson did you learn?	

Drafting: Shaping Your Writing

Using the following graphic organizer, map the events of your story in the order in which they occurred.

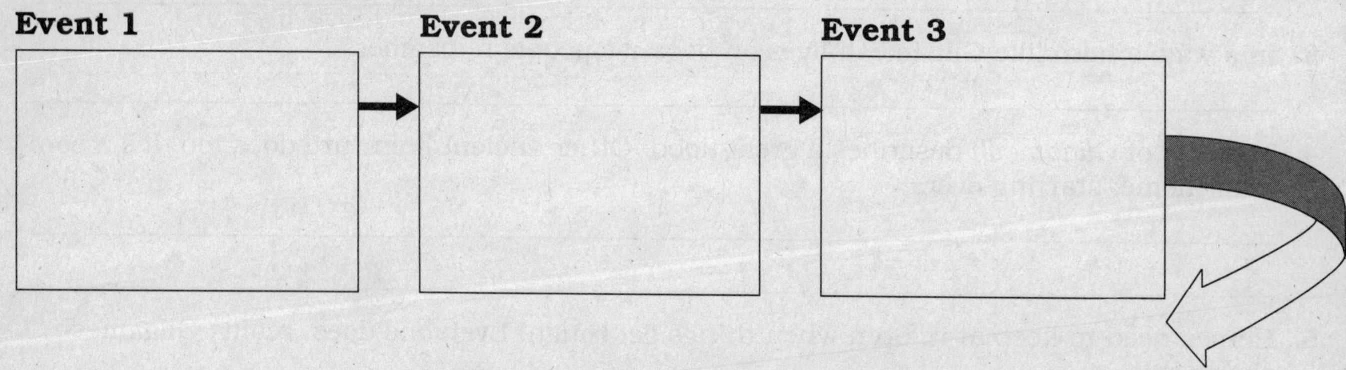

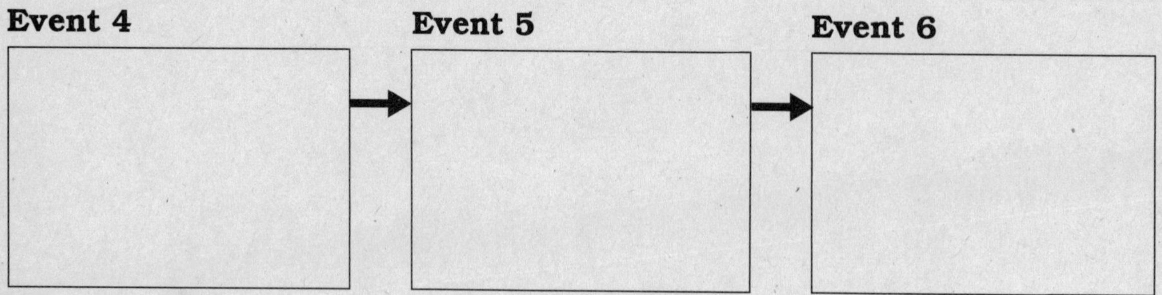

Name ______________________________ Date ______________

Writing Workshop—Unit 1

Autobiographical Narrative: Integrating Grammar Skills

Eliminating Unnecessary Tense Changes

Although your narrative may move back and forth in time, check to make sure that you have not changed verb tenses unnecessarily.

Incorrect: It *was* an hour after closing time, and I *am* still waiting.

Correct: It *was* an hour after closing time, and I *was* still waiting.

Fixing Incorrect Tense Changes

DIRECTIONS: *Rewrite the following sentences, correcting any unnecessary changes in verb tenses. If there are no errors in the sentence, write* correct.

1. The year I turned twelve, I grow ten inches.

____

2. When I wake up in the morning, I always splashed cold water on my face.

____

3. When I look at pictures in my yearbook, I thought about all the great times I've had with my friends in the past few years.

____

____

4. I was walking up the street when I suddenly see a mysterious blinking light in the bushes.

____

____

Name ______________________ Date ______________

Spelling—Unit 1

Proofreading Practice

DIRECTIONS: *Proofread the following passage, looking for twenty-six misspelled words. Cross out each misspelled word, and write it correctly in the space above.*

The *Egyptian Book of the Dead* was an important religeous text in the society of ancient Egypt. When wealthy Egyptians died, they were buried with a magnificant copy of this book, one that had been renderred by experienced scribes. The book contained numerous spells, conffesions, and words of power that served as a travel guide to the afterlife for departed souls.

The Egyptians believed that good deeds guaranted a person eaternal life. Rightious souls were redemed by Osiris, one of many gods worshipped by the Egyptians, and led into the afterlife. The evil souls of those who had sined, however, were tortured and destroied.

Ancient Egyptians believed that class divissions and social differances continued in the afterlife. That is why Egyptian faroahs were entombed in great pyramids filled with all their possesions. Thousands of workers toyled to build these well-enginered monuments of amazing dimensians. They laborred for decades, draging huge stone blocks up ramps and fiting them together. Fisicians embalmed the bodies of dead kings to preserve them for eaternity.

With their great pyramids, the ancient Egyptians left a signifficent, permanant mark on history.

Name ______________________________ Date ______________

Communications Workshop—Unit 1

Delivering a Speech

After choosing a topic, fill out the following chart to help you organize and present your speech.

Topic of speech: ______________________________

What is the main idea of your speech?
Who is the intended audience?
What details or examples are you using to support your ideas?
What visual aids (if any) do you plan to use?
What is the overall tone of your speech?

Name ______________________________ Date ______________

For Further Reading—Unit 1

DIRECTIONS: *Think about the books suggested for Unit 1 that you have read. Then, on a separate sheet of paper, answer the discussion questions and take notes for your literature circle.*

The Bible's Greatest Stories translated and retold by Paul Roche

Discussion Discuss the relationship between Ruth and Naomi. Why do you think Ruth feels such devotion for Naomi? Can you find modern examples that show the same degree of selflessness?

Connections—Literature Circle What major themes does the story of Noah explore? Why do you think the basic story has resonated so strongly with listeners and readers for hundreds of years?

Tales of Ancient Egypt selected and retold by Roger Lancelyn Green

Discussion Compare and contrast "The Girl with the Rose-red Slippers" with the version of the Cinderella story with which you are most familiar. How does each of the stories reflect its culture and era? What common values and characterizations do the two stories share?

Connections—Literature Circle Choose your favorite story from the collection. Explain to the group the elements of the story that you found particularly enjoyable or fascinating—plot, characterization, themes, or cultural beliefs.

The Epic of Gilgamesh translated by N. K. Sandars

Discussion The Gilgamesh legend is a story of the search for control in a chaotic world. Agree or disagree with this statement, using specific examples from the text to demonstrate your points.

Connections—Literature Circle Discuss the following idea: Does the Gilgamesh story have any relevance for modern readers? Support your opinion with specifics from the text and from your own knowledge and experience.

Early Irish Myths and Stories translated by Jeffrey Gantz

Discussion Geographically and economically, Ireland was once a land of hardships. Discuss the ways in which these myths and stories reflect the culture and environment in which they were written.

Connections—Literature Circle Myths were often written as explanations for natural phenomena. Choose one myth and discuss whether its explanation is logical.

The Conquest of New Spain by Bernal Díaz del Castillo, translated by J. M. Cohen

Discussion Firsthand accounts offer different views of historical events. Explain one event in this work that presented a view that surprised you. Use specifics from the text to support your explanation.

Connections—Literature Circle Describe the views that led the Spaniards to "conquer" the New World. Would these ideas be acceptable in today's society? Use specific examples from the text and your experience to support your answer.

ANSWERS

Unit 1 Introduction

Names and Terms to Know, p. 5

A. 1. F; 2. D; 3. C; 4. G; 5. E; 6. A; 7. H; 8. B

B. Sample Answers

1. The Sumerians developed Mesopotamia's earliest system of writing, called cuneiform.
2. In Egyptian religion, the pyramid was a symbol of the afterlife.
3. The Hebrews recorded their history in a sacred text now called the Bible.
4. Originally, Islam thrived as a religion of the poor in the area now known as Saudi Arabia.

Focus Questions, p. 6

Sample Answers

1. Before the advent of Hammurabi's code, there was no way to ensure consistency in the contracts and civil interactions that form the basis of commerce. In addition, the code made possible a more consistent definition of various crimes and the punishments to be prescribed for them; in general, justice, both civil and criminal, became far less arbitrary under the code than it had been before.
2. Because the Nile overflowed its banks every July, the surrounding soil was enriched, ensuring Egypt a prosperous farming economy. The Nile also provided a key waterway that promoted commerce and trade throughout the country.
3. The griot helped support the social order by speaking the praises of the ruler. By retelling the key events from the tribe's history and reciting poems and folk tales, the griot was the key to sustaining the tribe's cultural traditions.

Diagnostic Test 1, p. 2

MULTIPLE CHOICE

1. ANS: B
2. ANS: C
3. ANS: C
4. ANS: C
5. ANS: A
6. ANS: C
7. ANS: B
8. ANS: C
9. ANS: C
10. ANS: B
11. ANS: D
12. ANS: A
13. ANS: D
14. ANS: C
15. ANS: B

from *The Epic of Gilgamesh*

Vocabulary Warm-up Exercises, p. 8

A.
1. abundance
2. spawn
3. transformed
4. worldly
5. contend
6. extinguished
7. endowed
8. fulfilled

B. Sample Answers

1. Lemonade, soda, or milk would be a good *libation* for a children's birthday party.
2. I would probably feel very concerned and be torn between trying to see what was going on and wanting to get home.
3. News that my family was going to move to a different part of the country would make me *livid*.
4. If something were *amiss* between a friend and me, I would sit down and talk with him or her.
5. If the iron is *scorching*, it is burning hot, and could damage the clothes.
6. I would expect the repellent to keep insects away from me.
7. The colleagues of a *bailiff* would include police officers, attorneys, court reporters, and judges.
8. *Ballast* gives the ship weight and helps keep it from turning over.

Reading Warm-up A, p. 9

Sample Answers

1. Rivers would keep the soil wet, which is good for farming. A person might hope to be *endowed* with a talent for making money.
2. protecting the city-state; If a person *fulfilled* all of his or her responsibilities, the person might feel proud and ready for a break.
3. (plentiful); *Abundance* means "plenty."
4. They traded goods with other cultures; My grandparents are not very *worldly* because they have lived all their lives in a small town.
5. competition for territory and dominance; *Spawn* means "produce."
6. They were no longer independent; The brief snowfall *transformed* our street completely.
7. independence; An antonym for *extinguished* is *born*.
8. the culture of the Sumerian city-states became an important part of Babylonian society; *Contend* means "argue" or "maintain."

Reading Warm-up B, p. 10

Sample Answers

1. keeping order in a courtroom; The *bailiff* escorted the prisoner to his seat.
2. sparkling water; Many people's favorite *libation* is fruit-flavored sparkling water
3. using a low flame; The weather can be *scorching* in summer.
4. (noodles); *Ballast* means "weight that adds stability."
5. as we kids cheered and ran for the bowls; A traffic accident can create an *uproar.*
6. the surface of the baking dish with oil; Glenn *anointed* the dog's eyes with special drops.
7. (anger); A *livid* person has a red face.
8. One of the kids could have bumped into Grandpop, knocking the dish out of his hands. *Amiss* means "wrong."

Literary Analysis: Archetype—The Hero's Quest, p. 11

Hero: Gilgamesh

Purpose of quest: to attain immortality

Steps taken to reach goal: journeys through Manshu, travels across ocean to meet Utnapishtim, attempts to resist sleeping for six days and seven nights

Outcome: fails to attain immortality

Reading Strategy: Understand Cultural Context, p. 12

Sample Responses

1. Sumerians engraved on stone.
2. Sumerians used brick and cedar to build sturdy buildings.
3. Sumerians grew wheat.

Vocabulary Builder, p. 13

A. Using the Latin Prefix *sub-*

1. subtract
2. submarine
3. subtitles
4. subterranean
5. submerge

B. Using the Word List

1. ecstasy
2. teemed
3. babel
4. somber
5. succor

C. 1. A; 2. B; 3. D; 4. A

Grammar and Style: Commonly Confused Words *in* and *into,* p. 14

A. Practice

1. in
2. into
3. in
4. in
5. into
6. into
7. into

B. Writing Application

Sample Responses

1. Gilgamesh was a king in ancient times.
2. Gilgamesh went into the underworld to learn about immortality.
3. The people in Uruk were afraid of a giant.
4. Did the giant come into the city, or did it stay on the outskirts?
5. Humbaba lived in a cedar forest.
6. After going into the forest to fight Humbaba, Enkidu died from his wounds.

Enrichment: Epics and Epic Heroes, p. 17

Sample Responses

1. a great flood; the reign of Gilgamesh; the building of certain walls and temples
2. very high born—he is king, and part god
3. He saves people from the monster Humbaba, protects them in war, builds temples to their faith, and unsuccessfully tries to bring them the gift of immortality.
4. Values include strength, fighting prowess, courage, loyalty, friendship, curiosity, and faith. His flaws or limitations show his culture's recognition that immortality is impossible.
5. Responses will vary. Positive qualities and talents might include honesty, courage, love of freedom, democratic values, knowledge of science or computers, and skill with communicating, among many other things. Flaws might include arrogance or pride, among many other things.

Selection Test A, p. 18

Critical Reading

1. ANS: B	DIF: Easy	OBJ: Comprehension
2. ANS: D	DIF: Easy	OBJ: Literary Analysis
3. ANS: C	DIF: Easy	OBJ: Reading Strategy
4. ANS: A	DIF: Easy	OBJ: Reading Strategy
5. ANS: B	DIF: Easy	OBJ: Comprehension
6. ANS: C	DIF: Easy	OBJ: Interpretation
7. ANS: C	DIF: Easy	OBJ: Reading Strategy
8. ANS: C	DIF: Easy	OBJ: Literary Analysis
9. ANS: D	DIF: Easy	OBJ: Comprehension
10. ANS: A	DIF: Easy	OBJ: Interpretation
11. ANS: B	DIF: Easy	OBJ: Literary Analysis

Vocabulary and Grammar

12. ANS: A DIF: Easy OBJ: Vocabulary
13. ANS: C DIF: Easy OBJ: Vocabulary
14. ANS: C DIF: Easy OBJ: Grammar
15. ANS: B DIF: Easy OBJ: Grammar

Essay

16. Students should mention qualities such as courage, strength, loyalty, intelligence, compassion, and curiosity.
    Difficulty: *Easy*
    Objective: *Essay*
17. Students might mention weaknesses such as overconfidence and too much ambition. Students might note that having unrealistic goals is bound to result in disappointment.
    Difficulty: *Easy*
    Objective: *Essay*

Selection Test B, p. 21

Critical Reading

1. ANS: B DIF: Easy OBJ: Comprehension
2. ANS: D DIF: Easy OBJ: Interpretation
3. ANS: A DIF: Average OBJ: Reading Strategy
4. ANS: B DIF: Easy OBJ: Comprehension
5. ANS: C DIF: Average OBJ: Comprehension
6. ANS: A DIF: Challenging OBJ: Interpretation
7. ANS: A DIF: Challenging OBJ: Interpretation
8. ANS: C DIF: Easy OBJ: Literary Analysis
9. ANS: C DIF: Average OBJ: Literary Analysis
10. ANS: B DIF: Average OBJ: Comprehension
11. ANS: B DIF: Average OBJ: Literary Analysis
12. ANS: A DIF: Average OBJ: Interpretation
13. ANS: B DIF: Challenging OBJ: Literary Analysis
14. ANS: D DIF: Challenging OBJ: Literary Analysis
15. ANS: C DIF: Challenging OBJ: Reading Strategy

Vocabulary and Grammar

16. ANS: A DIF: Average OBJ: Vocabulary
17. ANS: A DIF: Easy OBJ: Vocabulary
18. ANS: D DIF: Average OBJ: Vocabulary
19. ANS: B DIF: Average OBJ: Grammar and Style
20. ANS: C DIF: Challenging OBJ: Grammar and Style

Essay

21. Students may mention courage, strength, loyalty, compassion, and a sense of responsibility as Gilgamesh's virtues. They may conclude that overconfidence and immodesty are his main flaws.
    Difficulty: *Easy*
    Objective: *Essay*
22. Students will most likely say that *Gilgamesh* fulfills the conditions of a quest story because it recounts the actions of a hero, Gilgamesh, who faces a series of challenges during his search for immortality: He journeys across the ocean to meet Utnapishtim, tries to resist sleeping for six days and seven nights, dives underwater to retrieve a special plant, and has the plant stolen by a serpent. They may also point out that Gilgamesh receives help from Utnapishtim and Urshanabi in striving to reach his goal.
    Difficulty: *Average*
    Objective: *Essay*
23. Students may discuss such values as wisdom, self-reliance, courage, friendship, loyalty, and devotion to the Sumerian gods and goddesses. From descriptions of Gilgamesh's and Utnapishtim's practice knowledge of building and construction, they may infer that Sumerians valued architecture and artisanry. Students should use examples from the selection to support their ideas.
    Difficulty: *Challenging*
    Objective: *Essay*

Genesis 1–3, "The Creation and the Fall," and 6–9, "The Story of the Flood"

Vocabulary Warm-up Exercises, p. 25

A.
1. expanse
2. devised (*also accept* created *or* fashioned)
3. created (*also accept* devised *or* fashioned)
4. midst
5. fashioned (*also accept* created *or* devised)
6. comprised
7. terminate
8. receded

B. Sample Answers
1. Grapes are grown in a vineyard.
2. *Maintain* means "to keep up." You need to be an honest and loyal friend in order to maintain good friendships.
3. Yes. *Array* means "an orderly arrangement." Options organized in an array make selection easier than would a random display.
4. I would like to see wild roses and daisies because they are my favorite flowers.
5. Yes. *Renown* means "fame." Almost everyone has seen the President's face in the media or has heard about the President in some way.
6. I need to plant it in suitable soil and water it regularly so that it will sprout, or grow quickly.

7. No. It is not worth cramming because you will probably forget most of the information before you take the test. It is better to study several days in advance so that you have time to learn and absorb the material on which you will be tested.
8. *Abound* means "to be plentiful." If I encounter many mosquitoes during my vacation, I would probably leave that place and stay somewhere else.

Reading Warm-up A, p. 26

Sample Answers

1. within this large area; The wide *expanse* of the plains made it difficult to search for the small birds.
2. the ark came to rest; After the waters *receded*, the ground was probably slimy and covered with debris.
3. (high altitude); *Created* means "produced."
4. in the middle of; We were in the *midst* of unpacking our suitcases when the doorbell rang.
5. (steep, rocky slopes); Last year, my garden *comprised* corn, tomatoes, peppers and squash.
6. Some people have hiked to the summit of Mount Ararat. *Devised* means "invented."
7. because of the difficulty and danger involved; The test will *terminate* promptly at five o'clock.
8. are encouraged by its mystery and their own eagerness to reach its peak; *Fashioned* means "formed."

Reading Warm-up B, p. 27

Sample Answers

1. (Planting; property; grapevines; land); We toured the *vineyard* and saw how grapes were grown there.
2. You need to examine your property, climate, water supply, soil quality, and the possibility of disease. A person might *maintain* a lawn or a rose garden.
3. that is growing on the land; *Vegetation* means "the plants of an area or region."
4. grape varieties that will be presented to you; The shoes were arranged in an orderly *array* according to size and color.
5. Just because you have heard of them; *Renown* means "fame."
6. rather than die; Those seeds will not *sprout* if you plant them when it is still cold outside.
7. There will be too many people who will be selling the products of their vineyards in the same place. *Abound* means "to be plentiful."
8. you will need it to meet your expenses; *Desirable* means "valuable" or "worth wanting or doing."

Literary Analysis: Archetypal Setting, p. 28

Sample Responses

Setting—paradise; *Details*—Garden of Eden, place of no toil for Adam and Eve, full of lush plants

Setting—universe made up of opposites; *Details*—day and night, sky and water, sun and moon, land and sea, plants and animals, all of which are detailed in the opening of Genesis

Setting—landscape that emerges from dark or watery emptiness or confusion; *Details*—world and heavens created out of the void

Setting—giant tree that connects heaven and earth; *Details*—such a tree found in center of Garden of Eden

Setting—great flood and ship that survives it;

Details—great flood from forty days of rain; Noah's ark with his family and two of every kind of animal

Reading Strategy: Identify Chronological Order, p. 29

A. 2, 7, 4, 8, 5, 1, 6, 3

B. Sample response: When humanity became evil, God decided to destroy his creation in a great flood. Because Noah was the one righteous man, God told Noah how to survive the flood in an ark that he was to build for his family and two of every kind of beast. Then God made it rain for forty days, and water covered the Earth. Then, to check to see whether the waters had subsided, Noah sent out several birds. In the end, he and the others in the ark survived the great flood.

Vocabulary Builder, p. 30

A. Using the Prefix *com-*

Sample Responses

1. the act of considering what two or more things they have in common
2. someone accompanying someone else
3. feeling; concern
4. going well together
5. to speak with; to share ideas

B. Using the Word List

1. duped
2. corrupt
3. comprise
4. void
5. expanse

C. 1. C; 2. A; 3. B

Grammar and Style: Punctuation in Dialogue, p. 31

A. Practice

1. When did God say, "Let there be light"?
2. "Let the earth bring forth every kind of living creature," God said.
3. After creating Adam and Eve, God told them, "Fill the earth and master it."
4. The serpent asked Eve, "Did God really say not to eat of that tree?"

B. Writing Application

Sample Dialogue

1. "God is going to destroy Earth in a flood!" Noah exclaimed.
2. "How terrible!" cried his wife.
3. Noah told her, "Only those who come on the ark with me will be saved."
4. "What ark?" asked his wife.
5. "The one I am building in accordance with the Lord's instructions," Noah replied.

Enrichment: Science, p. 34

Sample Responses

1. It would look more like a lizard because it still had limbs. God punished it later by removing its limbs and condemning it to slinking along without them.
2. From the story, people may associate snakes with evil or deception.
3. Possible reasons include their odd limbless appearance, their startling speed, their hissing sound, and their swallowing their prey whole.
4. They eat insects, rodents, and other pests that harm farm crops and spread disease.
5. Yes; they are coldblooded and get their heat from the environment, instead of generating it in their bodies as warmblooded creatures do. In cold weather, there would not be enough heat for the snakes, so hibernating would be helpful for survival.

Selection Test A, p. 35

Critical Reading

1. ANS: D	DIF: Easy	OBJ: Literary Analysis
2. ANS: A	DIF: Easy	OBJ: Reading Strategy
3. ANS: D	DIF: Easy	OBJ: Reading Strategy
4. ANS: B	DIF: Easy	OBJ: Literary Analysis
5. ANS: C	DIF: Easy	OBJ: Interpretation
6. ANS: C	DIF: Easy	OBJ: Literary Analysis
7. ANS: D	DIF: Easy	OBJ: Interpretation
8. ANS: A	DIF: Easy	OBJ: Comprehension
9. ANS: A	DIF: Easy	OBJ: Comprehension
10. ANS: B	DIF: Easy	OBJ: Comprehension
11. ANS: D	DIF: Easy	OBJ: Literary Analysis
12. ANS: C	DIF: Easy	OBJ: Vocabulary
13. ANS: B	DIF: Easy	OBJ: Vocabulary
14. ANS: B	DIF: Easy	OBJ: Grammar
15. ANS: B	DIF: Easy	OBJ: Grammar

Essay

16. Some students might blame the serpent because the beast deceived Eve, who was very innocent. Other students might blame Eve, arguing that she should have known that the word of God should come before that of a serpent.

Difficulty: *Easy*

Objective: *Essay*

17. Students should mention that God at first is unforgiving about human evil and destroys humanity with a great flood. After the flood, God is willing to see the human race grow. God's attitude might have changed because Noah kept his obligation to God.

Difficulty: *Easy*

Objective: *Essay*

Selection Test B, p. 38

Critical Reading

1. ANS: D	DIF: Average	OBJ: Literary Analysis
2. ANS: A	DIF: Easy	OBJ: Reading Strategy
3. ANS: C	DIF: Average	OBJ: Reading Strategy
4. ANS: C	DIF: Average	OBJ: Interpretation
5. ANS: A	DIF: Easy	OBJ: Literary Analysis
6. ANS: B	DIF: Average	OBJ: Interpretation
7. ANS: C	DIF: Challenging	OBJ: Interpretation
8. ANS: D	DIF: Challenging	OBJ: Comprehension
9. ANS: D	DIF: Easy	OBJ: Comprehension
10. ANS: A	DIF: Easy	OBJ: Interpretation
11. ANS: B	DIF: Average	OBJ: Literary Analysis
12. ANS: D	DIF: Average	OBJ: Reading Strategy
13. ANS: B	DIF: Challenging	OBJ: Interpretation
14. ANS: D	DIF: Average	OBJ: Comprehension
15. ANS: C	DIF: Challenging	OBJ: Literary Analysis

Vocabulary and Grammar

16. ANS: C	DIF: Easy	OBJ: Vocabulary
17. ANS: A	DIF: Average	OBJ: Vocabulary
18. ANS: D	DIF: Challenging	OBJ: Vocabulary
19. ANS: A	DIF: Average	OBJ: Grammar and Style
20. ANS: C	DIF: Challenging	OBJ: Grammar and Style

Essay

21. Students should recognize that Eden is a lush place with an abundance of food to be had with minimal toil. They should cite key details, such as the tree of life, the tree of knowledge, the river that waters the garden, and the four branches of the river.

Difficulty: *Easy*

Objective: *Essay*

22. Students should recognize God's general bounty, illustrated in his creating humanity in his image and giving them a paradise at Eden; his rewards to human beings who are pious, as Noah is; and his punishment when his commands are disobeyed, as when he sends Adam

and Eve from Eden and destroys all of humanity, leaving only Noah and his family to survive.

Difficulty: *Average*

Objective: *Essay*

23. In addition to the creation, students may note that the selection explains the reason the Sabbath is observed, the reason human beings must work, the reason snakes are considered evil, and the reason serpents have no limbs.

Difficulty: *Challenging*

Objective: *Essay*

The Book of Ruth Psalms 8, 19, 23, and 137

Vocabulary Warm-up Exercises, p. 42

A. 1. splendor
2. adorned
3. inflicted
4. prosper
5. morsel
6. abiding
7. molest
8. steadfast

B. Sample Answers

1. A kindergarten student might give his or her *handiwork* to his or her parents.
2. I would look for information about someone who is *deceased* in the obituary section of the local newspaper.
3. If I *dominate* in a sport, my opponents may be afraid of me.
4. If I *withheld* my judgment, then I did not express my opinion.
5. Every bird hatches from an egg, so every bird was *formerly* an egg.
6. I would confront the person who *perpetuated* the rumor and ask him or her to apologize to my friend.
7. In order to *sustain* good grades, I need to continue to complete my homework.
8. If there is radio *interference*, I will hear static.

Reading Warm-up A, p. 43

Sample Answers

1. luxury; I think the Grand Canyon is an example of *splendor* in nature.
2. (silk ribbons); (embroidery); I adorned my hair with a lovely barrette.
3. (not find enough steady employment); (the money they had began running out); A person would want to prosper so that he or she could live a comfortable life.
4. They could barely afford what they needed. A *morsel* is a very small amount.
5. a cruel form of punishment; The students *inflicted* cruelty on Ana because she did not fit in.
6. (suffered); *Molest* means "disturb or annoy."
7. (From the time she was a small child); *Abiding* means "long-lasting."
8. always loyal and faithful; *Steadfast* means "constant" or "unwavering."

Reading Warm-up B, p. 44

Sample Answers

1. (today); My favorite actor was *formerly* a guitar player in a rock band.
2. through scripture in the Bible; A story can be *perpetuated* if someone bases a movie on it.
3. died out; The daughter of the *deceased* woman inherited the family home.
4. The Moabites grew their own food and raised sheep. A modern person might *sustain* himself or herself by opening a store and living off the profit from the store.
5. The Moabites dominated in wool production. I *dominate* the basketball court whenever I get the ball.
6. Two types of handiwork may include embroidery or pottery. *Handiwork* means "anything made by a particular person."
7. brought the stories to light; My mother *withheld* her judgment until I could tell her my side of the story.
8. (brought an end to their independence); The *interference* of the linebacker prevented me from scoring.

Literary Analysis: Parallelism, p. 45

Sample Responses

1. "The heavens declare the glory of God, / the sky proclaims His handiwork"; Psalm 19:2
2. "Day to day makes utterance, / night to night speaks out"; Psalm 19:3
3. "His rising-place is at one end of heaven, / and his circuit reaches the other"; Psalm 19:7. "Only goodness and steadfast love shall pursue me all the days of my life, / and I shall dwell in the house of the LORD for many long years"; Psalm 23:6
4. "The man's name was Elimelech, his wife's name was Naomi, and his two sons were named Mahlon and Chilion"; Ruth 1:2. "Their voice car ries throughout the earth, / their words to the end of the world"; Psalm 19:5

Reading Strategy: Use Context Clues, p. 46

Sample Responses

1. prevent, block; *context clue*—"should you wait for them to grow up?"
2. reward, payment; *context clue*—"reward"
3. take part, join; *context clue*—"At mealtime," "dip your morsel"
4. continue; *context clue*—"that the name of the deceased may not disappear"

5. something spoken, a remark; *context clue*—"speaks out"
6. smear ceremonially; *context clue*—"my head with oil"
7. roof of the mouth; *context clue*—"let my tongue stick to"

Vocabulary Builder, p. 47

A. Using the Anglo-Saxon Root *-stead-*

1. in place of
2. place where a farm is
3. place at the head of a bed
4. remaining in place

B. Using the Word List

1. avenger
2. precepts
3. glean
4. redeem
5. lucid
6. steadfast
7. reapers

C. 1. B; 2. A; 3. D

Grammar and Style: Compound Predicates, p. 48

A. Practice

Conjunctions are italicized.

1. During a famine, Naomi's family came to the land of the Moabites *and* remained there.
2. Naomi lost her family *and* was left with two sons.
3. Both of Naomi's sons married Moabites married *but* then died too.
4. The daughters-in-law could remain with the Moabites *or* go with Naomi back to Judah.
5. Orpah, unlike Ruth, stayed with her people *and* did not accompany Naomi.

B. Writing Application

Sample responses (conjunctions are italicized):

1. At first, Ruth was branded an outsider *and* treated badly.
2. Then Boaz recognized her loyalty *and* ensured better treatment.
3. Following Naomi's instructions, she went to Boaz *and* slept at his feet.
4. Mahlon's closest male relative could redeem Ruth through marriage *or* allow Boaz to marry her.
5. In the end she married Boaz *and* became the great-grandmother of King David.

Enrichment: Marriage Laws and Practices, p. 51

1. B
2. C
3. B
4. A
5. D
6. A
7. C
8. B
9. C

Selection Test A, p. 52

Critical Reading

1. ANS: C	DIF: Easy	OBJ: Interpretation
2. ANS: D	DIF: Easy	OBJ: Reading Strategy
3. ANS: A	DIF: Easy	OBJ: Interpretation
4. ANS: B	DIF: Easy	OBJ: Literary Analysis
5. ANS: B	DIF: Easy	OBJ: Reading Strategy
6. ANS: D	DIF: Easy	OBJ: Comprehension
7. ANS: A	DIF: Easy	OBJ: Interpretation
8. ANS: C	DIF: Easy	OBJ: Comprehension
9. ANS: D	DIF: Easy	OBJ: Literary Analysis
10. ANS: A	DIF: Easy	OBJ: Reading Strategy
11. ANS: C	DIF: Easy	OBJ: Comprehension
12. ANS: B	DIF: Easy	OBJ: Comprehension

Vocabulary and Grammar

13. ANS: C	DIF: Easy	OBJ: Vocabulary
14. ANS: B	DIF: Easy	OBJ: Vocabulary
15. ANS: A	DIF: Easy	OBJ: Grammar

Essay

16. Most students will recognize that in the Book of Ruth, loyalty is portrayed positively. Naomi is loyal to her daughters-in-law; in return, Ruth remains loyal to Naomi. Ruth remains loyal to her family by working dutifully for Boaz, and Boaz shows his gratitude to Ruth by remaining loyal to her when he strikes a deal with the town elders to sell the family's land.

    Difficulty: *Easy*

    Objective: *Essay*

17. Students should recognize that Ruth shows great loyalty and sacrifices a great deal to remain with Naomi and to live among Naomi's people. She also volunteers to perform manual labor in Boaz's fields. Students might further note that Ruth remains just as loyal to Boaz in the second half of the story as she was to Naomi, so her character remains basically the same throughout—thinking more about others than about herself.

    Difficulty: *Easy*

    Objective: *Essay*

Selection Test B, p. 55

Critical Reading

1. ANS: C	DIF: Average	OBJ: Comprehension
2. ANS: D	DIF: Easy	OBJ: Literary Analysis

3. ANS: C DIF: Challenging OBJ: Literary Analysis
4. ANS: D DIF: Challenging OBJ: Interpretation
5. ANS: A DIF: Average OBJ: Reading Strategy and Literary Analysis
6. ANS: D DIF: Easy OBJ: Comprehension
7. ANS: B DIF: Average OBJ: Interpretation
8. ANS: B DIF: Challenging OBJ: Interpretation
9. ANS: A DIF: Average OBJ: Comprehension
10. ANS: C DIF: Average OBJ: Reading Strategy
11. ANS: C DIF: Challenging OBJ: Literary Analysis
12. ANS: B DIF: Challenging OBJ: Reading Strategy
13. ANS: B DIF: Easy OBJ: Interpretation

Vocabulary and Grammar

14. ANS: C DIF: Average OBJ: Vocabulary
15. ANS: D DIF: Easy OBJ: Vocabulary
16. ANS: D DIF: Average OBJ: Grammar
17. ANS: C DIF: Challenging OBJ: Grammar

Essay

18. Students should recognize that Ruth displays great loyalty to her deceased husband's mother and sacrifices a great deal to be with Naomi and adopt her ways. They may speculate about the combination of motives that drive her—love of her deceased husband, desire to help her mother-in-law, insistence on keeping promises, and a seeming conversion to Jewish ways. Students should cite details from the Bible story to illustrate their general statements about Ruth.

    Difficulty: *Easy*

    Objective: *Essay*

19. Students should recognize that the Book of Ruth contains characters, settings, themes, and a plot that centers on one or more conflicts. They should identify as the conflict Ruth's and Naomi's desire to find happiness after their great bereavement. Students should discuss some of the myriad setting details about agriculture, ancient Jewish laws and customs, and the landscape and peoples of biblical times. They should mention that the story conveys themes about loyalty, love, suffering and redemption, and the treatment of foreigners. They should recognize that the characters' problems and the setting help make the story realistic.

    Difficulty: *Average*

    Objective: *Essay*

20. Students should cite examples of parallelism in which the parallel portions complete, negate, repeat, or otherwise elaborate on the earlier portions of the verses. Students should show how the parallelism helps stress or enhance important ideas, especially the concept of God's power and glory in the first three psalms. Some students may also discuss how parallelism contributes to the powerful rhythm of the psalms, thereby making them more poetic and memorable.

    Difficulty: *Challenging*

    Objective: *Essay*

from the *Qur'an*

Vocabulary Warm-up Exercises, p. 59

A.
1. relieved
2. guidance
3. renown
4. compassionate
5. charity
6. affliction
7. endeavors
8. resume

B. **Sample Answers**
1. If my pet went *astray*, I would go look for it.
2. I would pack *varied* types of clothing for a trip so that I could dress for the weather.
3. Yes, if someone recognized the fact that I did a good job, I would be pleased.
4. It is important to be *merciful* to a person in need because people should help one another through trouble.
5. If I *incurred* a great loss, I might file a claim with the insurance company to help replace what was damaged.
6. A person who *created* a movie about baseball would probably need access to a ballpark or a set built like a ballpark in order to film scenes recreating the game.
7. I *abhor* candy, then I will not buy myself a candy bar.
8. I would need to use good *judgment* because severe weather conditions might make traveling unsafe.

Reading Warm-up A, p. 60

Sample Answers
1. All Muslims and many non-Muslims know about it; Bill Murray is a person of great *renown*.
2. if they haven't enough money, or if they are suffering from illness or a serious affliction; *Relieved* means "freed from."
3. (illness); The itchy spots on his arm indicated that he was suffering from a strange affliction.
4. Muslim teaching; *Guidance* means "advice or direction."
5. projects; I dismissed my other *endeavors* and concentrated completely on tennis.
6. giving it to the poor; He showed great *charity* by volunteering to help the elderly.
7. merciful; *Compassionate* means "full of sympathy."
8. return home; usual lives; The play will resume after the intermission has ended.

Reading Warm-up B, p. 61

Sample Answers

1. containing different types of writing; Its *varied* colors made the painting pleasing to observe.
2. their own order for the text; *Created* means "produced."
3. (from the path of righteousness); Our mission went *astray* because we didn't follow orders.
4. rewarded; The referee gave his *judgment*, and the player was benched.
5. (Compassionate); John's merciful act of giving food to the stray dog helped the animal survive.
6. because they think that these translations poorly express the teachings; I *abhor* sweet drinks because I prefer a tarter taste.
7. the obligation to read it in the original Arabic; *Incurred* means "took on."
8. The scholars are gratified to study the surahs because they discover the beauty and inspiration that the surahs contain. *Gratified* means "pleased" or "satisfied."

Literary Analysis: Imagery, p. 62

Sample Responses

1. *Senses*—sight, touch; *Concept*—right behavior; *Effect*—makes life seem a journey
2. *Sense*—sight; *Concept*—nightfall; *Effect*—makes Night seem like a woman letting down her hair
3. *Senses*—sight, touch; *Concept*—punishment; *Effect*—takes you by surprise because "smooth the path" sounds positive, and *affliction* is shocking
4. *Senses*—sight, touch; *Concept*—the ultimate punishment; *Effect*—creates a concrete image of Hell
5. *Sense*—sight; *Concept*—the Lord's compassion to humans in need; *Effect*—makes Allah sound like a sympathetic and kindly protector, an adopted father

Reading Strategy: Set a Purpose for Reading, p. 63

1. Students should quote or otherwise identify the sentences that were most relevant to their purpose.
2. Students should summarize or paraphrase the information that is most relevant to their purpose.
3. Sample narrowed purposes: to learn more about the times Muslims pray each day or the requirements for almsgiving

Vocabulary Builder, p. 64

A. Using the Latin Prefix *ab-*

1. abdicate; 2. abolish; 3. absolve

B. Using the Word List

1. C; 2. D; 3. A; 4. E; 5. B

C. 1. A; 2. C; 3. A

Grammar and Style: Parallelism, p. 65

A. Practice

Sample Responses

1. Muhammad continued receiving revelations from the age of forty until his death.
2. Surahs vary in length from three or four verses to more than 200 verses.
3. Muhammad is viewed not as the author but as the transmitter of Allah's message.
4. Correct

B. Sample response: Above all, I value my family, my home, and my country.

Enrichment: Islamic Art, p. 68

Sample Responses

1. Highly representational art is discouraged in the Qur'an, out of the concern that it might encourage idol-making.
2. Calligraphy is ornamental writing. It is central to Islamic art because the written word is so important and highly esteemed in Islam.
3. abstract geometric patterns and natural patterns such as flowers and vines
4. The stylized drawing would be more patterned and artificial and would probably emphasize symmetry and geometrical elements in the flower's shape.
5. to create beauty for over 1000 years
6. from the seventh century through the eighteenth century

Selection Test A, p. 69

Critical Reading

1. ANS: D	DIF: Easy	OBJ: Reading Strategy
2. ANS: C	DIF: Easy	OBJ: Comprehension
3. ANS: A	DIF: Easy	OBJ: Literary Analysis
4. ANS: B	DIF: Easy	OBJ: Interpretation
5. ANS: A	DIF: Easy	OBJ: Literary Analysis
6. ANS: C	DIF: Easy	OBJ: Comprehension
7. ANS: B	DIF: Easy	OBJ: Literary Analysis
8. ANS: B	DIF: Easy	OBJ: Reading Strategy
9. ANS: C	DIF: Easy	OBJ: Comprehension
10. ANS: D	DIF: Easy	OBJ: Reading Strategy
11. ANS: C	DIF: Easy	OBJ: Interpretation

Vocabulary and Grammar

12. ANS: B	DIF: Easy	OBJ: Vocabulary
13. ANS: A	DIF: Easy	OBJ: Vocabulary
14. ANS: C	DIF: Easy	OBJ: Grammar
15. ANS: B	DIF: Easy	OBJ: Grammar

Essay

16. Students should note that these readings from the Qur'an emphasize both God's mercy and his justness.

The passages imply that those who worship the Lord and carry out his will through good works will be rewarded; those who stray from his path will be punished.

Difficulty: *Easy*

Objective: *Essay*

17. Students might note that "Night" appeals to the senses of touch, smell, and sight when it speaks of punishment in the afterlife as "blazing Fire." "The Exordium" appeals to the sense of sight when it portrays right behavior as "the straight path."

    Difficulty: *Easy*

    Objective: *Essay*

Selection Test B, p. 72

Critical Reading

1. **ANS:** A	**DIF:** Easy	**OBJ:** Comprehension
2. **ANS:** C	**DIF:** Easy	**OBJ:** Literary Analysis
3. **ANS:** C	**DIF:** Average	**OBJ:** Interpretation
4. **ANS:** B	**DIF:** Easy	**OBJ:** Comprehension
5. **ANS:** B	**DIF:** Average	**OBJ:** Reading Strategy
6. **ANS:** A	**DIF:** Average	**OBJ:** Literary Analysis
7. **ANS:** D	**DIF:** Average	**OBJ:** Literary Analysis
8. **ANS:** A	**DIF:** Average	**OBJ:** Comprehension
9. **ANS:** A	**DIF:** Average	**OBJ:** Interpretation
10. **ANS:** C	**DIF:** Easy	**OBJ:** Comprehension
11. **ANS:** A	**DIF:** Average	**OBJ:** Reading Strategy

Vocabulary and Grammar

12. **ANS:** B	**DIF:** Average	**OBJ:** Vocabulary
13. **ANS:** A	**DIF:** Easy	**OBJ:** Vocabulary
14. **ANS:** D	**DIF:** Average	**OBJ:** Vocabulary
15. **ANS:** A	**DIF:** Average	**OBJ:** Vocabulary
16. **ANS:** D	**DIF:** Average	**OBJ:** Grammar and Style
17. **ANS:** C	**DIF:** Easy	**OBJ:** Grammar and Style

Essay

18. Students should note that the readings from the Qur'an emphasize God's mercy on the one hand and his justice on the other. Those who do the Lord's will and behave righteously will be rewarded; those who disbelieve and do not do God's will are to be punished.

    Difficulty: *Easy*

    Objective: *Essay*

19. Students should describe the meaning and effect of one of the concrete images from the passages in the Qur'an that they read. For example, the straight path is a recurring image that refers to virtuous conduct. The fact that such behavior is pictured as a path suggests that Muslims are envisioned as being on a journey with a destination. They could be lost if they strayed from the path, which is mapped out by the Word of the Lord in the Qur'an.

    Difficulty: *Average*

    Objective: *Essay*

20. Sample purposes (in addition to the ones suggested in the question): to learn more about righteous behavior; to learn more about how sinners are to be punished; to learn more about how the good are to be rewarded; to see what other concrete images the Qur'an uses to portray abstract ideas

    Difficulty: *Challenging*

    Objective: *Essay*

from *The Thousand and One Nights:* "The Fisherman and the Jinnee"

Vocabulary Warm-up Exercises, p. 76

A.
1. jinn
2. bestow .
3. consequences
4. resolutely
5. lamentations
6. Doubtless
7. venom
8. resumed

B. Sample Answers

1. Motive means "a reason for action." I want to save enough money to buy a car.
2. One proverb, or "wise saying," that inspires me is "Where there is a will, there is a way."
3. I would like to predict an end to world hunger.
4. No. If I embrace, or hug, someone who has a cold, I will probably get a cold from that person.
5. The nicest aspect, or part, of my personality is my sense of humor.
6. No. I would not need a plentiful amount of supplies for days' worth of camping.
7. I need to make the effort to study.
8. Arteries are important because they carry blood away from the heart.

Reading Warm-up A, p. 77

Sample Answers

1. firmly made up his mind; Courage and firmness can help a person act resolutely.
2. sadly; Lamentations means "expressions of sorrow or grief."
3. grant me a few wishes; The jinn granted the girl's wish.
4. It was covered by the evening news, and it was reported in all of today's papers; Doubtless means "certainly."
5. I arrived too late for my job interview; Consequences means "results."

6. (start again); Pam resumed her walk after the speeding car passed by her.
7. cobra; There is no antidote for that snake venom.
8. luck; Bestow means "to give."

Reading Warm-up B, p. 78

Sample Answers

1. (many); The bounteous food on the table was prepared for the celebration.
2. (human or animal); A rainstorm has more than one aspect. It can be gloomy and uncomfortable if you are walking in it, but it can actually feel cozy if you are watching it from inside.
3. to make Aladdin get a magic lamp for him; Motive means "reason for an action."
4. Despite his efforts; Sarah was honored for her endeavors in finding a cure for cancer.
5. (predicted); The prophet told us that a mysterious woman would enter our lives in the future.
6. Ask and you shall receive; Proverb means "a wise saying."
7. because it is the symbol of having dreams comes true; Embrace means "to hug or to hold."
8. as the blood travels through arteries in the body; The arteries in our bodies serve a very important function.

Literary Analysis: Folk Tales, p. 79

Sample Responses

1. Those who show mercy are treated mercifully; those who do not are not.
2. All of the characters have only one or two traits. For example, the fisherman is poor and clever; the jinnee is faithless and cruel; King Sindbad is ungrateful; the falcon is loyal.
3. the jinnee, the falcon, Duban the Doctor's revenge
4. The fisherman is good and the jinnee is evil; Duban the Doctor is good, and the king's vizier is evil; the falcon is good.
5. The fisherman tricks the powerful jinnee into getting back into the bottle; Duban the Doctor gets revenge on the powerful king.

Reading Strategy: Summarize, p. 80

Sample Responses

Main Idea or Event: Fisherman finds bottle; *Supporting Details:* fisherman is fishing; fisherman casts net far out; fisherman gets jinnee's bottle in net.

Main Idea or Event: Jinnee vows to kill whoever releases him; *Supporting Details:* jinnee's evil past; vow to bestow riches on whoever frees him; change in vow when no one frees him

Main Idea or Event: Fisherman outsmarts jinnee; *Supporting Details:* Fisherman says he doesn't believe that bottle held jinnee and gets jinnee to prove it did by reentering bottle; fisherman seals bottle and throws bottle with jinnee back into the sea.

Vocabulary Builder, p. 81

A. Using the Latin Root *-vert-*

1. someone who is turned inward; someone who is not outgoing or friendly
2. someone who is turned outward to the world; an outgoing, friendly person
3. the feeling of turning and turning; dizziness
4. to turn to something else; to change to another course or philosophy; also, a person who makes such a change
5. to turn back; to return to an earlier form, view, or position

B. Using the Word List

1. T; 2. F; 3. F; 4. T; 5. T

C. 1. B; 2. C; 3. B; 4. A; 5. A

Grammar and Style: Action Verbs and Linking Verbs, p. 82

A. Practice

1. tossed, A
2. felt, L
3. hauled, A
4. felt, A

B. Writing Application

Sample Responses

1. The fisherman was poor.
2. Duban the Doctor looked at King Yunan's leprosy.
3. The jinnee looked huge and scary.
4. With the seal off the bottle, the jinnee appeared in a cloud of smoke.
5. The king grew angrier and angrier at the poor bird.

Enrichment: Supernatural Creatures, p. 85

1. He once offered great wealth but now he brings death.
2. He is in a bottle, imprisoned there by King Solomon after refusing to accept Solomon's faith.
3. Responses should recognize that he takes on a giant version of human form.
4. The fisherman tricks the jinnee into going back into the bottle, whereupon he throws the bottle back into the sea. He reaps no material benefits. The outcome might suggest that there are no short cuts to success and happiness; that brains can trump strength and even supernatural powers; and that life is full of surprises.
5. Among other things, students may suggest that such creatures give human beings a supernatural explanation for their own impotence and so bring them comfort when things go wrong; that such creatures anthropomorphize bad luck or injustice in a way that makes it easier to accept; that such creatures help explain things

that seemed or seem inexplicable; and/or that such creatures are simply entertaining because their existence and behavior play with the bounds of reality in imaginative ways.

Selection Test A, p. 86

Critical Reading

1. ANS: B	DIF: Easy	OBJ: Literary Analysis
2. ANS: B	DIF: Easy	OBJ: Literary Analysis
3. ANS: D	DIF: Easy	OBJ: Interpretation
4. ANS: D	DIF: Easy	OBJ: Literary Analysis
5. ANS: A	DIF: Easy	OBJ: Literary Analysis
6. ANS: D	DIF: Easy	OBJ: Comprehension
7. ANS: C	DIF: Easy	OBJ: Reading Strategy
8. ANS: C	DIF: Easy	OBJ: Reading Strategy
9. ANS: A	DIF: Easy	OBJ: Literary Analysis
10. ANS: B	DIF: Easy	OBJ: Reading Strategy
11. ANS: A	DIF: Easy	OBJ: Comprehension

Vocabulary and Grammar

12. ANS: C	DIF: Easy	OBJ: Vocabulary
13. ANS: D	DIF: Easy	OBJ: Vocabulary
14. ANS: C	DIF: Easy	OBJ: Grammar
15. ANS: D	DIF: Easy	OBJ: Grammar

Essay

16. King Yunan finds that he has leprosy. Soon a wise old doctor named Duban arrives and announces to the king that he can cure the disease. After the cure proves successful, the king is so grateful that he showers gifts and personal attention on Duban. A wicked vizier, jealous of the king's fondness for the doctor, convinces the king that someone who can cure him could also kill him. The king recalls the story of a king who killed a falcon that was trying to save his life. Later, however, the king gives in to his fear and decides to kill the doctor. The king is then poisoned because he follows the doctor's final instructions.

    Difficulty: *Easy*

    Objective: *Essay*

17. Students should note the selection's life lessons. They may say that the tale teaches the importance of not giving in to frustration and not blaming people for problems they did not create. Students may also note that kindness is not always repaid with kindness.

    Difficulty: *Easy*

    Objective: *Essay*

Selection Test B, p. 89

Critical Reading

1. ANS: A	DIF: Average	OBJ: Literary Analysis
2. ANS: A	DIF: Average	OBJ: Interpretation
3. ANS: B	DIF: Easy	OBJ: Comprehension
4. ANS: C	DIF: Challenging	OBJ: Reading Strategy
5. ANS: C	DIF: Average	OBJ: Interpretation
6. ANS: D	DIF: Average	OBJ: Comprehension
7. ANS: D	DIF: Average	OBJ: Comprehension
8. ANS: B	DIF: Easy	OBJ: Interpretation
9. ANS: B	DIF: Challenging	OBJ: Literary Analysis
10. ANS: B	DIF: Average	OBJ: Reading Strategy
11. ANS: B	DIF: Average	OBJ: Literary Analysis
12. ANS: A	DIF: Average	OBJ: Literary Analysis
13. ANS: D	DIF: Challenging	OBJ: Interpretation
14. ANS: A	DIF: Easy	OBJ: Comprehension
15. ANS: C	DIF: Challenging	OBJ: Literary Analysis

Vocabulary and Grammar

16. ANS: C	DIF: Easy	OBJ: Vocabulary
17. ANS: B	DIF: Average	OBJ: Vocabulary
18. ANS: C	DIF: Easy	OBJ: Grammar
19. ANS: A	DIF: Challenging	OBJ: Grammar and Style
20. ANS: D	DIF: Average	OBJ: Grammar and Style

Essay

21. Students should include the following information: When King Yunan has leprosy, Duban tells him of an amazing way to cure it, and the king is grateful. Later a jealous vizier points out that a man clever enough to cure the king so miraculously could also kill him in an equally amazing way. The vizier recommends that the king execute the doctor. The king, recalling the story of King Sindbad and the falcon, at first refuses, but the vizier is persuasive, and the king changes his mind. The doctor begs for mercy and declares that if he is killed, the king will also be killed, but the king does not need him. The doctor begs to be given a day in which to put his affairs in order, and he promises to give the king a book of mysteries. Just before his death, the doctor presents the book to the king, instructing him to turn its pages after Duban's death. Duban is put to death, and the king is killed by poison the doctor had left on the pages of the book.

    Difficulty: *Easy*

    Objective: *Essay*

22. Students should discuss at least three of the following: characters with only one or two traits, ordinary characters who outsmart or trick more powerful characters, magical or supernatural elements, a clear distinction between good and evil, and a message or moral offering a lesson about life.

    Difficulty: *Average*

Objective: *Essay*

23. Students should recognize that all three stories stress the need for mercy and for repaying kindness with kindness, loyalty with loyalty. The jinnee and the two kings fail to recognize kindness or loyalty, repay them unfairly, and in the end either meet their downfall or, in the case of King Sindbad, experience great regret.

Difficulty: *Challenging*

Objective: *Essay*

Benchmark Test 1, p. 92

MULTIPLE CHOICE

1. ANS: A
2. ANS: C
3. ANS: C
4. ANS: B
5. ANS: B
6. ANS: B
7. ANS: A
8. ANS: D
9. ANS: C
10. ANS: B
11. ANS: B
12. ANS: A
13. ANS: D
14. ANS: A
15. ANS: D
16. ANS: C
17. ANS: C
18. ANS: D
19. ANS: A
20. ANS: C
21. ANS: D
22. ANS: C
23. ANS: A
24. ANS: B
25. ANS: D
26. ANS: D
27. ANS: B
28. ANS: A

ESSAY

29. Students should provide an extended definition that clarifies the role of heroism in present-day society. Then, based on that definition, they should compare and contrast the role and quest of a contemporary action hero with a hero from ancient literature, using specific, concrete examples to illustrate their points.
30. Students can choose the biblical passage of their choice, preferably one with a narrative structure that allows them to respond to a concrete story line. In writing about their reaction to the biblical narrative, they should focus their remarks on the extent to which the passage offers useful guidance about behavior in the contemporary world, using concrete examples to support their arguments.
31. Students should do more than just give opinions about the work in question: they should explain why specific elements of the work succeed or fail, and they should support their judgments with specific examples and clear reasoning.

Diagnostic Test 2, p. 98

MULTIPLE CHOICE

1. ANS: C
2. ANS: D
3. ANS: B
4. ANS: C
5. ANS: A
6. ANS: B
7. ANS: D
8. ANS: C
9. ANS: A
10. ANS: B
11. ANS: D
12. ANS: A
13. ANS: C
14. ANS: D
15. ANS: C

from the *Rubáiyát* by Omar Khayyám
from the *Gulistan:* from "The Manners of Kings" by Sa'di

Vocabulary Warm-up Exercises, p. 102

A.
1. destined
2. mystics
3. Whilst
4. enthusiastically
5. diminished
6. assailing
7. oppression
8. beneficent

B. Sample Answers
1. Yes, I would be *pacified,* or satisfied, with an apology, if the apology were sincere.
2. Happiness is more important to me. You cannot put a monetary price on happiness. *Prosperity* cannot buy happiness.

3. A consequence, or *result*, of lying to my best friend would be that would be unable to trust me—and that she might no longer wish to be my friend.
4. If I *dispersed* flower seeds in the ground, flowers might later bloom in the places where the seeds were scattered.
5. It is important to keep *oneself* healthy in order to enjoy life and complete daily activities.
6. Even though my friend and I like to eat different foods, we could meet at the cafeteria and bring our own lunches.
7. One type of weather that can cause a *calamity* is a hurricane.
8. If a person tried to *oppress* me, I would report his or her behavior to the appropriate authorities.

Reading Warm-up A, p. 103

Sample Answers

1. to rule an empire in Central Asia and the Middle East; *Destined* means "fated."
2. used military force to control their subjects; forced their subjects to convert to a form of Islam that did not include mystics; *Whilst* I was in school, my mother prepared my surprise party.
3. No, mystics were not part of the form of Islam practiced by the Seljuks. *Mystics* means "spiritual people."
4. Because of this persecution; The regime's *oppression* of free speech forced the publishers to sell that book in another country.
5. Many Iranians organized themselves to overthrow the Seljuks; *Diminished* means "decreased."
6. excitement about their cause; The boy read *enthusiastically* from his favorite magazine.
7. driving them out of Iran; *Assailing* means "assaulting."
8. he was treated with the respect that a ruler deserves; *Beneficent* means "kind."

Reading Warm-up B, p. 104

Sample Answers

1. calmed; We *pacified* the growling dog by giving it something to eat.
2. Sufis care more about direct personal experience with God than about *prosperity* or possessions.
3. some religions are based on logic; the Sufi mystics think that a person needs knowledge that comes from inspiration; John likes to visit Florida, *whereas* I prefer to vacation in Alaska.
4. (various disciplines); One should always dress *oneself* appropriately, depending on the weather.
5. they will grow closer to God; *Consequence* means "result."
6. (various peoples all over the world); The congregation *dispersed* after the memorial service ended.
7. stop them from practicing their religion; It is unjust to *oppress* a person who is weaker than you are.
8. (cultural); *Calamity* means "disaster."

Literary Analysis: Didactic Literature, p. 105

Sample Responses

A. Lesson: A power-hungry person, one who is hungry to exploit others, like a wolf, cannot be a just and successful ruler, because he devours rather than guards what he rules over.

Present-day or personal application: Dictators who oppress their subjects often find that the people will eventually revolt and overthrow them.

B. Lesson: Don't loll about in bed—a new day is an exciting opportunity to do something special.

Present-day or personal application: Sometimes it's easy to let a day just slip away without making the most of what it offers.

C. Lesson: Time moves on and writes our life's script—nothing will allow you to go back and change a single moment of what's past.

Present-day or personal application: Make the most of life and plan ahead because mistakes made today can never be reversed.

Reading Strategy: Break Down Long Sentences, p. 106

A sample rephrasing follows each broken-down sentence:

1. "The helpless fellow began to insult the king on that occasion of despair, with the tongue | he had, | and to use foul expressions according to the saying: | *Who washes his hands of life* | *Says whatever* | *he has in his heart*." The helpless man, in despair, began to insult the king, using foul language. His situation was like the one described in this saying: The person who has no hope left says what is on his mind.
2. "The Wordly Hope | men set their Hearts upon | Turns Ashes— | or it prospers; and anon, / Like Snow upon the Desert's dusty Face, / Lighting a little hour or two—is gone." The hope that people have either fades or grows. If it grows, it soon becomes like snow in the desert: After a short time, it disappears.
3. "The vizier asked the king how | it came to pass that | Feridun, | who possessed neither treasure nor land nor a retinue, | established himself upon the throne." The vizier asked the king how it could be that Feridun—who had nothing—became king.

Vocabulary Builder p. 107

A. Using the Latin Root *-tort-*

Sample responses (students should also define the words): contortion; contortionist; contort; distort; distortion; extort; extortion; extortionist; retort; torture; tortuous

B. Using the Word List

1. pomp; 2. repentance; 3. extortions

C. 1. B; 2. A; 3. A

Grammar and Style: Interjections p. 108

A. Practice

1. Well, look at what we have here.
2. Yea! Our team finished first in the finals.
3. No! Don't say that.
4. Alas, I never reached my goal.
5. Oh my! This is so exciting.

B. Writing Application

Sample Answer

Picture this! A book of poetry read under a tree, some crusty French bread, a bottle of wine—and, best of all, you! What a slice of slice of heaven that would be!

Enrichment: World Languages, p. 111

Sample Responses

1. Students might mention that computers, modems, fax machines, and airplanes have made the world seem smaller. The technology of television has been especially powerful in bringing images of people from other countries into living rooms. Students should support their opinions about whether the world should become smaller.
2. Students might mention clothing, cars, electronic equipment, and food. If a business sets up a factory or office in another country, all people working for that business should learn the language of that country so that business can be conducted smoothly. Trade with other countries has also increased.
3. Whenever people get to know each other on a one-on-one basis, prejudices tend to disappear. If people throughout the world were better able to communicate, they might not feel so different from one another. People would be able to learn about different ideas and customs.

Selection Test A, p. 112

Critical Reading

1. ANS: D	DIF: Easy	OBJ: Literary Analysis
2. ANS: D	DIF: Easy	OBJ: Literary Analysis
3. ANS: C	DIF: Easy	OBJ: Interpretation
4. ANS: A	DIF: Easy	OBJ: Reading Strategy
5. ANS: D	DIF: Easy	OBJ: Literary Analysis
6. ANS: B	DIF: Easy	OBJ: Interpretation
7. ANS: A	DIF: Easy	OBJ: Comprehension
8. ANS: D	DIF: Easy	OBJ: Comprehension
9. ANS: C	DIF: Easy	OBJ: Literary Analysis
10. ANS: A	DIF: Easy	OBJ: Reading Strategy
11. ANS: D	DIF: Easy	OBJ: Literary Analysis

Vocabulary and Grammar

12. ANS: B	DIF: Easy	OBJ: Vocabulary
13. ANS: C	DIF: Easy	OBJ: Vocabulary
14. ANS: A	DIF: Easy	OBJ: Grammar
15. ANS: A	DIF: Easy	OBJ: Grammar

Essay

16. Students may say that experience is a good teacher, on the basis of things they have learned personally. They may also say that those who tell the truth are not always kind.
    Difficulty: *Easy*
    Objective: *Essay*
17. Students may note that because poems have rhythm and rhyme, it is easier to remember the lessons taught. They may also say that poetry was simply the usual form and that either prose or poetry could serve the purpose of teaching a lesson.
    Difficulty: *Easy*
    Objective: *Essay*

Selection Test B, p. 115

Critical Reading

1. ANS: B	DIF: Average	OBJ: Literary Analysis
2. ANS: B	DIF: Easy	OBJ: Comprehension
3. ANS: A	DIF: Average	OBJ: Interpretation
4. ANS: C	DIF: Average	OBJ: Comprehension
5. ANS: B	DIF: Average	OBJ: Literary Analysis
6. ANS: A	DIF: Easy	OBJ: Comprehension
7. ANS: A	DIF: Easy	OBJ: Literary Analysis
8. ANS: C	DIF: Average	OBJ: Literary Analysis
9. ANS: A	DIF: Challenging	OBJ: Reading Strategy
10. ANS: C	DIF: Challenging	OBJ: Reading Strategy
11. ANS: D	DIF: Average	OBJ: Comprehension

Vocabulary and Grammar

12. ANS: C	DIF: Easy	OBJ: Vocabulary
13. ANS: D	DIF: Average	OBJ: Vocabulary
14. ANS: A	DIF: Challenging	OBJ: Vocabulary
15. ANS: D	DIF: Average	OBJ: Vocabulary
16. ANS: C	DIF: Average	OBJ: Grammar and Style
17. ANS: B	DIF: Challenging	OBJ: Grammar and Style

Essay

18. Students should state their opinion of the statement and provide examples and reasons to back it up. They may say that it is wrong to avoid the truth even if doing so causes trouble, because greater trouble could be caused by lies and illusions. Alternatively, they may agree that when telling the truth would be only hurtful or dangerous, it is better to avoid the truth.

Difficulty: *Challenging*

Objective: *Essay*

19. Students will most likely focus on *The Rubáiyát* because a number of the verses express ideas and emotions about the brevity of life in colorful, eloquent language. For example, the poet refers to earth as a "Caravanserai" and the sultan's sojourn on it as just an hour. Life is also described as a cup to be filled and drunk. The poet focuses on earthly life, which is short, but paints it in sensuous, sweet terms.

Difficulty: *Average*

Objective: *Essay*

From the Translator's Desk

Coleman Barks Introduces the Poetry of Rumi, p. 118

1. Barks first became acquainted with Rumi's poetry in 1976, when he was thirty-nine years old. Barks's friend, poet Robert Bly, introduced Barks to Rumi's poetry and said that the Persian writer's poems needed "to be released from their cages."
2. He sat at the restaurant drinking hot tea, and he worked on translating a poem by Rumi.
3. Barks recalls the time when, at the age of six, he had made a specialty of memorizing the capitals of all the world's countries. The Latin teacher stumped him, though, by naming the ancient region of Cappadocia, which had no capital city marked on modern maps. Barks learned that the most important city of Cappadocia was Iconium (later Konya), which is where the poet Rumi lived and was buried.
4. Barks seems to mean that what a person does not know—even more than what he or she knows—is central to that person's existence and personality.
5. The word *springs* connotes sacredness, and the word *fountain* connotes artificiality.
6. He speculates that Rumi must be fulfilling a need or longing of the soul.
7. Answers will vary. Encourage students to support their choice of criteria with reasons and examples.

Coleman Barks

Listening and Viewing, p. 119

Sample answers and guidelines for evaluation:

Segment 1: Coleman Barks believes that the scholars who had previously translated Rumi's poems did not have a good sense of the madness of the poems. The translators were not poets but scholars and they were unable to understand the works from a poet's sensibility. By translating the poems into free verse, Coleman has brought them to a greater audience.

Segment 2: Coleman Barks believes that Rumi's poems introduce new ideas that are expressed in conversational form and touch on intense themes, such as love, to which everyone can relate. Students may answer that Rumi's poetry is important today because he writes about universal themes that people of all cultures can relate to, allowing Rumi's work to be a "healing" voice in today's conflicted world.

Segment 3: When Coleman Barks translates, he must remove his own voice and tell Rumi's truth; when Coleman Barks writes his own poetry, he uses his voice to tell the truth in his own way. Students may say that in order for a translator to be accurate, he or she must write from the point of view of the original poet or writer.

Segment 4: Barks thinks that it is important to learn about other cultures in order to become a "global self"—a person who knows what is going on in the world and is able to metabolize it. Students may suggest that they could learn about the customs of other cultures, the era that Rumi lived in, and more about themselves by being able to relate to the emotion and themes in Rumi's work.

"Elephant in the Dark," "Two Kinds of Intelligence," "The Guest House," and "Which Is Worth More" by Rumi

Vocabulary Warm-up Exercises, p. 121

A.
1. genuine
2. acquired
3. grateful
4. preserved
5. malice
6. conduits
7. depression
8. intelligence

B. Sample Answers

1. Cartoons are not based on *reality.* All kinds of things happen in them that would never happen in real life.
2. My CD collection is worth *preserving.*
3. A person who cheats does not behave *honorably.*
4. If water is *overflowing,* I can turn off the faucet and pull out the stopper in the drain.
5. I prefer to study in *solitude* so that there are no distractions.
6. The water flowing in a river is moving, so it is not *stagnant.*
7. I have *competence* in chess.
8. You must have *awareness* when you cross a street; otherwise, you might be struck by a car.

Reading Warm-up A, p. 122

Sample Answers

1. (true); *Genuine* designer clothes are more expensive than imitations.
2. might have been forgotten; *Preserved* means "protected."

3. (a special importance among many Muslim groups); *Acquired* means "obtained possession of."
4. The ideas that flow through Rumi's poetry; Gutters are *conduits* for water in the street after a heavy rain.
5. (he has also preserved their cultural history in the *Masnavi*); If you are *grateful* to someone, you should remember to thank that person."
6. this work; *Intelligence* means "power of understanding."
7. kindness; I do not like people who hold a grudge or act with *malice.*
8. (uplifting); (inspiring); The fact that our favorite baseball team won the World Series lifted my friends and me out of our *depression.*

Reading Warm-up B, p. 123

Sample Answers

1. keeping it alive; A photo album is one way of *preserving* memories.
2. (isolated); When some people want *solitude*, they take a hike in the mountains.
3. it is very difficult and structured; Playing professional basketball requires great *competence.*
4. appearance; A cartoon shows a fantasy, not *reality.*
5. (it gets faster); *Stagnate* means "turn unhealthy or unpleasant because of a lack of movement."
6. (the dervishes spin faster); It is important to have *awareness* when you are driving.
7. (spill out); The washing machine was *overflowing*, so we called the repair person.
8. respect; *Honorably* means "with respect."

Literary Analysis: Analogy, p. 124

Sample Answers

1. The unfamiliar—or in this case, mysterious—matter that is being explained is the soul—especially the inner workings of the soul.
2. The unfamiliar thing—the soul, or the inner workings of the soul—is likened to a guest house, which is a more familiar concept, one that is easier to "get your mind around."
3. The comparison helps in understanding the soul because it show how thoughts and moods kind of just present themselves, in a way that is often beyond our will—they just sort of show up and depart suddenly, like uninvited people in a guest house. And just as we can learn something from all people, even those we don't like or admire, so we can learn something from the less-than-happy or admirable thoughts or feelings that pass through the "house" of our soul.

Reading Strategy: Make Generalizations, p. 125

Sample Response

Students might note the following: "Elephant in the Dark"—generalization: Each individual sees only part of the truth (supporting details: each person in the poem, as he/she feels the elephant in the dark, gets a different, partial impression of what it is [one thinks it's like a water-pipe, another like a column, another a throne, etc.]). "Two Kinds of Intelligence"—generalization: Each of us has a kind of limited intelligence learned in school, which helps us succeed in practical ways (details: "you rise in the world," "you get ranked or behind others," "competence in retaining information"), and another, more intuitive, unlimited intelligence that comes from within and that gives us personal wisdom (details: "a spring overflowing its springbox," "a freshness in the center of your chest," "a fountainhead moving from within you"). "The Guest House"—generalization: The soul is like a guest house that receives visitors in the form of widely varying moods and thoughts, all of which should be received graciously because they all have something to teach us (details: "every morning a new arrival," "a joy, a depression, a meanness," "invite them in"). "Which Is Worth More"—generalization: Time spent alone is more valuable than time spent in a crowd (details: "a crowd of thousands," "your own genuine solitude," "alone in your room," "more valuable than anything else").

Vocabulary Builder, p. 126

A. Using the Prefix *com-* or *con-*

Rumi's poetry communicates profound truths by combining sound and sense so seamlessly that each word perfectly complements every other word.

B. Using the Word List

1. C; 2. B; 3. C; 4. A

C. 1. A; 2. C; 3. B; 4. D

Grammar and Style: Agreement and the Indefinite Pronouns *each* and *no one,* p. 127

A. Practice

1. No one here [has] ever seen an elephant.
2. Each of us [touches] one place.
3. Each one of them [is] a new arrival.
4. Each [has] been sent as a guide from the beyond.
5. No one [knows] which guest might come to your door.

B. Writing Application

1. According to Rumi, each of your moods has its value.
2. Rumi believes that no one of us can know the full extent of the truth on his [or *her*] own.
3. No one can be the complete master of her [or *his*] fate.
4. Each person who has sat alone meditating in a room knows the value of moments of solitude.
5. Each of you possesses an infinite store of wisdom inside if you will only search for it.

Enrichment: Sufism, p. 130

Sample Responses

Light images: he who possesses a torch of his own; That leader is his own director and light; illuminated one; from that light whereon his soul is nourished; Knows the wise man to be the light of his eyes; He has no lamp which wherewith to light himself; nor half a lamp which might recognize and seek light

Throughout this poem, the image of light is almost synonymous with wisdom. The wise man has his own torch—his inherent wisdom; the half-wise, who has no torch of his own, follows the wise man's light; the fool has no lamp but doesn't have the sense to realize that he is stumbling in the dark. These light images create the picture of human existence as a murky and dangerous enterprise. Only the wise can find their way through it on their own.

Selection Test A, p. 131

Critical Reading

1. ANS: C DIF: Easy OBJ: Comprehension
2. ANS: C DIF: Easy OBJ: Literary Analysis
3. ANS: A DIF: Easy OBJ: Reading Strategy
4. ANS: A DIF: Easy OBJ: Reading Strategy
5. ANS: D DIF: Easy OBJ: Interpretation
6. ANS: B DIF: Easy OBJ: Literary Analysis
7. ANS: C DIF: Easy OBJ: Literary Analysis
8. ANS: B DIF: Easy OBJ: Comprehension
9. ANS: A DIF: Easy OBJ: Literary Analysis
10. ANS: D DIF: Easy OBJ: Reading Strategy

Vocabulary and Grammar

11. ANS: A DIF: Easy OBJ: Vocabulary
12. ANS: C DIF: Easy OBJ: Vocabulary
13. ANS: C DIF: Easy OBJ: Grammar
14. ANS: A DIF: Easy OBJ: Grammar
15. ANS: B DIF: Easy OBJ: Grammar

Essay

16. Students should note that "Elephant in the Dark" and "Two Kinds of Intelligence" discuss the idea of seeing many sides. "The Guest House" advises people to be open to thoughts and feelings. "Which Is Worth More?" urges readers to look inward for truth.

    Difficulty: *Easy*

    Objective: *Essay*

17. Some students will argue that great power would enable someone to do much good for many people. Others might argue that power can also be used to harm people and that the only way to develop wisdom is to spend time alone with your thoughts.

    Difficulty: *Easy*

    Objective: *Essay*

Selection Test B, p. 134

Critical Reading

1. ANS: B DIF: Average OBJ: Interpretation
2. ANS: D DIF: Challenging OBJ: Reading Strategy
3. ANS: B DIF: Easy OBJ: Literary Analysis
4. ANS: C DIF: Easy OBJ: Comprehension
5. ANS: A DIF: Challenging OBJ: Reading Strategy
6. ANS: A DIF: Challenging OBJ: Literary Analysis
7. ANS: A DIF: Average OBJ: Literary Analysis
8. ANS: D DIF: Average OBJ: Reading Strategy
9. ANS: A DIF: Average OBJ: Comprehension
10. ANS: B DIF: Easy OBJ: Comprehension
11. ANS: B DIF: Average OBJ: Literary Analysis
12. ANS: A DIF: Challenging OBJ: Comprehension
13. ANS: D DIF: Average OBJ: Reading Strategy
14. ANS: B DIF: Average OBJ: Literary Analysis
15. ANS: A DIF: Average OBJ: Interpretation

Vocabulary and Grammar

16. ANS: C DIF: Average OBJ: Vocabulary
17. ANS: A DIF: Easy OBJ: Vocabulary
18. ANS: B DIF: Challenging OBJ: Vocabulary
19. ANS: A DIF: Easy OBJ: Grammar
20. ANS: C DIF: Challenging OBJ: Grammar

Essay

21. Students' responses should compare the use of metaphor in two poems and should use examples to support the greater effectiveness of the use of metaphor in one of the poems.

    Difficulty: *Average*

    Objective: *Essay*

22. Students may see an apparent contradiction. "Elephant in the Dark" implies that only with others can we gain the enlightenment needed to perceive truth. "Which Is Worth More?" stresses the value of solitude. Students may also note, however, that even though some of our deepest perceptions might spring from within, it is only by interacting with others that we can gain enough experience to inspire a thirst for inner wisdom.

    Difficulty: *Challenging*

    Objective: *Essay*

African Proverbs
from *Sundiata: An Epic of Old Mali*

Vocabulary Warm-up Exercises, p. 138

A.
1. memories
2. preparations
3. journey
4. enormous
5. lively
6. latter
7. foolish

8. experience

B. Sample Answers

1. There might be fatigue, perspiration, and relief; applause might be heard.
2. No, the Empire State Building is a human-made structure.
3. Yes. *Likewise* means "also."
4. No, the Fourth of July is a not an average day; it is a national holiday. *Ordinary* means "average" or "usual."
5. If someone hoped to become a professional golfer and won his or her first golf tournament at an early age, person believe to be golfing is his or her destiny.
6. You will not express your feelings at all. *Buried* means "covered from view."
7. Capitals usually have a legislative building where representatives meet to make laws.
8. You would make the changes soon as possible. *Henceforth* means "from now on."

Reading Warm-up A, p. 139

Sample Answers

1. (trip); I'd like to make a journey to the Great Lakes.
2. (plan ahead); In the morning, people make *preparations* such as packing lunch or choosing a good outfit to wear.
3. They should have *experience* in safely guiding tourists in Africa. *Experience* means "skill or knowledge gained through participation."
4. may give you a chance to rest more peacefully after a busy day sightseeing; *Latter* means "the second of two."
5. (animated); The little girl kept us amused with her *lively* personality.
6. elephants, rhinoceroses, and giraffes; *Enormous* means "immense."
7. not to take along a broad-brimmed hat and sunscreen; *Foolish* means "silly."
8. It is an exotic travel experience that is really like no other; *Memories* means "remembrances."

Reading Warm-up B, p. 140

Sample Answers

1. secrets forever hidden; I think the pyramids of Egypt are one of the great *mysteries* of the world.
2. Timbuktu was a spiritual capital for Islamic thought and culture during the fifteenth and sixteenth centuries. *Likewise* means "also."
3. People came from as far away as Saudi Arabia to study there. As a result, many great mosques, schools, and libraries were built in Timbuktu; *Capital* means "the city that is the official seat of government."
4. merchant ships; *Competed* means "tried to win something that others are also trying to win."
5. Muslim scholars still go there to study; the sand of the Sahara is threatening the city; *Ordinary* means "average" or "usual."
6. many historical buildings; The pirates *buried* their treasure on the beach.
7. of being swallowed up by the desert; *Destiny* means "fate."
8. It must be protected from the windblown sands of the Sahara. *Henceforth* means "from now on."

Literary Analysis: Epic Conflict and Proverbs, p. 141

A. Sample Responses

1. *Example*—Sogolon Djata and his mother after Sassouma Bérété humiliates her over the baobab leaf; *Resolution*—Sogolon Djata uproots the baobab tree and gives it to his mother.
2. *Example*—Sogolon Djata is ridiculed by the other people in his community because he does not walk; *Resolution*—At last, Sogolon Djata uses the iron bar to stand up and walk.
3. *Example*—He realizes that his mother has been hurt because of his own laziness and taciturn nature;
   Resolution—He makes the decision to walk.

B. Sample Response

Proverb—Eyes do not see all. (Zulu)

Application to Sogolon Djata—The people who see only Sogolon Djata's deformed appearance and his inability to walk underestimate his inner strength, which he shows first when he accepts his father's declaration that he will be king and then, conclusively, when he decides to walk.

Application to Present-Day Life—What we see on the surface is not the whole reality and may be misleading. For instance, the images we see on television may be only partially true and may even have been manipulated to present false information.

Reading Strategy: Reread for Clarification, p. 142

1. Naré Maghan is speaking to his son, Mari Djata; *Passage*—"One day Naré Maghan made Mari Djata come to him and he spoke to the child."
2. the father of Doua; *Passage*—"Doua's father was my father's griot."
3. Balla Fasséké; *Passage*—"the son of Doua, Balla Fasséké here, will be your griot."
4. the history of his ancestors and the art of governing; *Passage*—"you will hear the history of your ancestors, you will learn the art of governing Mali."

Vocabulary Builder, p. 143

A. Using the Latin Root *-firm-*

1. infirmary
2. confirmation
3. affirmation
4. firmament

B. Using the Word List

1. C; 2. A; 3. D; 4. F; 5. G; 6. E; 7. B

C. Sample Sentences

1. The malicious journalist, almost diabolical in his viciousness and his cleverness, made an innuendo that damaged the candidate's chances in the election.
2. The fact that he was taciturn led him to become estranged from members of his family because he seemed not to care about them.
3. Her infirmity included a number of symptoms whose cause the physician was at a loss to fathom.

Grammar and Style: Sentence Variety, p. 144

A. Practice

Sample Sentences

1. At the age of three, Sogolon's son could only crawl; prepositional phrases
2. When Sogolon heard gossip about her son, she became frustrated; subordinate clause
3. Often proverbs find lessons for human behavior in the animal world; adverb

B. Writing Application

Sample Revision

After the death of Naré Maghan, Sogolon suffered. Spitefully, Sassouma Bérété banished Sogolon and her son to a backyard of the palace. How miserable Sogolon was! Would her son ever walk? In order to ease his mother's pain, Sogolon Djata promised to walk. When he kept his promise, people were shocked.

Enrichment: Geography, p. 147

Sample Responses

1. Most people live in the southern part of Mali, where most cities are located. It is a more fertile, livable area.
2. He probably lived in southern Mali.
3. Algeria
4. Mopti
5. the Senegal River; Kayes and Bafoulabe

Selection Test A, p. 148

Critical Reading

1. ANS: C	DIF: Easy	OBJ: Literary Analysis
2. ANS: D	DIF: Easy	OBJ: Reading Strategy
3. ANS: D	DIF: Easy	OBJ: Comprehension
4. ANS: C	DIF: Easy	OBJ: Reading Strategy
5. ANS: C	DIF: Easy	OBJ: Literary Analysis
6. ANS: A	DIF: Easy	OBJ: Interpretation
7. ANS: A	DIF: Easy	OBJ: Interpretation
8. ANS: B	DIF: Easy	OBJ: Comprehension
9. ANS: B	DIF: Easy	OBJ: Literary Analysis
10. ANS: B	DIF: Easy	OBJ: Interpretation
11. ANS: B	DIF: Easy	OBJ: Reading Strategy

Vocabulary and Grammar

12. ANS: D	DIF: Easy	OBJ: Vocabulary
13. ANS: A	DIF: Easy	OBJ: Vocabulary
14. ANS: D	DIF: Easy	OBJ: Grammar
15. ANS: C	DIF: Easy	OBJ: Grammar

Essay

16. Students should describe the conflicts their hero faces, how that hero overcomes them, and how Sogolon Djata is similar to or different from their hero.

    Difficulty: *Easy*

    Objective: *Essay*

17. Students might note that Sogolon Djata cannot walk; his father is disappointed in him; he is rejected by society; his mother reproaches him; and, finally, he must face a test of strength. The conflict with society prevents him from achieving his kingship before this event.

    Difficulty: *Easy*

    Objective: *Essay*

Selection Test B, p. 151

Critical Reading

1. ANS: C	DIF: Challenging	OBJ: Reading Strategy
2. ANS: B	DIF: Easy	OBJ: Literary Analysis
3. ANS: D	DIF: Easy	OBJ: Literary Analysis
4. ANS: B	DIF: Easy	OBJ: Interpretation
5. ANS: C	DIF: Average	OBJ: Comprehension
6. ANS: B	DIF: Average	OBJ: Reading Strategy
7. ANS: A	DIF: Challenging	OBJ: Interpretation
8. ANS: A	DIF: Average	OBJ: Literary Analysis
9. ANS: C	DIF: Challenging	OBJ: Literary Analysis
10. ANS: C	DIF: Challenging	OBJ: Comprehension
11. ANS: B	DIF: Average	OBJ: Interpretation

Vocabulary and Grammar

12. ANS: D	DIF: Average	OBJ: Vocabulary
13. ANS: C	DIF: Average	OBJ: Vocabulary
14. ANS: C	DIF: Easy	OBJ: Grammar and Style
15. ANS: A	DIF: Average	OBJ: Grammar and Style
16. ANS: D	DIF: Average	OBJ: Grammar and Style

17. ANS: D DIF: Challenging OBJ: Grammar and Style

Essay

18. Students should describe conflicts between Sogolon Djata and the other people of his village, who mock him for not walking; between Sogolon Djata and his mother on the one hand and Sassouma on the other, as Sassouma humiliates Sogolon and Sogolon Djata; between Sogolon and Sogolon Djata, as Sogolon expresses her resentment over his failure to stand up for her. Students should also describe the internal conflict that takes place within Naré Maghan as he considers his son's suitability to become a good king. Finally, they should describe the conflict taking place within Sogolon Djata over his own course of action, implied in the fact that he rarely speaks, seldom smiles, and does not do much until finally stirred by his mother's despair. These conflicts make Sogolon Djata a strong king because they teach him to be patient, to deal with adversity, and to develop inner strength.

    Difficulty: *Average*

    Objective: *Essay*

19. Students should explain the meaning of the proverb, analyze what it reveals about the African society that generated it, and then apply it to contemporary American society. Sample response: The proverb about chasing two gazelles means that you cannot have two competing goals; you must choose one to pursue. The proverb reveals that the culture values common sense and the ability to focus on one problem at a time. It also suggests that hunting is an important part of the culture. The proverb's relevance to contemporary society might be that you cannot be committed both to making as much money as possible and to devoting your energies to your family.

    Difficulty: *Challenging*

    Objective: *Essay*

Writing About Literature—Unit 1

Analyze Literary Periods: Integrating Grammar Skills, p. 155

Sample Revisions

1. Like the heroes of other cultural epics and even like today's movie heroes, Gilgamesh values bravery, loyalty, and heroic deeds.
2. Failing in his quest for eternal life, Gilgamesh must finally accept his own mortality. This hard-won lesson is one that every human being must learn.
3. Although Gilgamesh must die, his name and spirit live on as people recount his heroic deeds.
4. Like many ancient literary works, the epic of *Gilgamesh* describes the destruction of the world in a great flood and the beginning of a new creation. This theme of the gods destroying the world by flood and then recreating it is common in ancient literature from around the world.
5. One value that the epic of *Gilgamesh* demonstrates is the need for human perseverance. Like Gilgamesh, every person needs to overcome great challenges without giving into despair, in order to accomplish great deeds.

Writing Workshop—Unit 1

Autobiographical Narrative: Integrating Grammar Skills, p. 157

1. The year I turned twelve, I grew two inches.
2. When I wake up in the morning, I always splash cold water on my face.
3. When I look at pictures in my yearbook, I think about all the great times I've had with my friends in the past few years.
4. I was walking up the street when I suddenly saw a mysterious blinking light in the bushes.

Spelling—Unit 1

Proofreading Practice, p. 158

1. important; 2. religious; 3. magnificent; 4. rendered;
5. confessions; 6. guaranteed; 7. eternal;
8. Righteous; 9. redeemed; 10. worshiped; 11. sinned;
12. destroyed; 13. divisions; 14. differences;
15. pharoahs; 16. possessions; 17. toiled;
18. engineered; 19. dimensions; 20. labored;
21. dragging; 22. fitting; 23. Physicians; 24. eternity;
25. significant; 26. permanent